PACE Academy

M000206816

SCARS OF LOVE

Tears of Hope

By

Deborah Goforth

With

Mark Graham

Scars of Love, Tears of Hope
by Deborah Goforth with Mark Graham

Copyright © 2007 Deborah Goforth

All rights reserved. No part of this book may be reproduced or transmitted
in any form or by any means, electronic or mechanical, including
photocopying, recording or by any information storage and retrieval
system, without permission from the author, except for the inclusion
of brief quotations in review.

ISBN Number 13: 978-0-9796458-0-8

Library of Congress Control Number: 2007903996

First Edition: August, 2007

Cover and Book design: Nick Zelinger, www.nzgraphics.com

Published by At-Risk Educational Services

Visit our Web site at www.studentsatrisk.com

Printed in the United States of America

Note:
Throughout *Scars of Love*,
the names of children have been changed.

This book is dedicated to:

My father and My Hero, Roland (Sarge) Goforth

Thank you for making me the person I am today.

By teaching me life lessons, encouraging me to take care of those who can not or will not care for themselves, and to stand up for those who are less fortunate, you have made all of this possible.

Acknowledgments

I am the person I am today because of the love and support of a wonderful family and remarkable friends. Hugs and Kisses to David, Dorinda, Jordan, Hayden, John, Alia, Kris, Phyllis, Donny, Danine, Cody, Marissa, Damon, and most important my father and mother, Sarge and Barbara Goforth.

Julia Gonzalez, you are the best friend anyone in the world could have. I am so very blessed to have you in my life, and I treasure our friendship.

Nathaniel Slawson, you are a remarkable man, and I am so fortunate to call you my friend. You are one of my "Keepers of Hope."

Always and Forever Terry.

Robin Dehnel and Charlotte Dehnel, I would like to thank you for your amazing friendship and the gentle shove at lunch that day, pushing me to write this book.

Jennifer Feck, I am so glad I was selected to be your mentor many years back because it has turned into a wonderful friendship.

Thank goodness technology brought me such an amazing friend as Charlyn Doyle.

To an astonishing man, Chief Savoie, thank you for your morning hug that always started my day, for your unwavering support when I was tired, and for your prayers of strength and encouragement. Thanks to Chief and Keith Aguirre for sharing the excitement of writing a book with me. Good luck with yours.

I would like to thank four women for their friendship but also for pushing me to grow professionally: Billie Halbert, Jackie Shepperson, Sue VanHoozer, and Marty Jonas.

Margie Ridgeway and Jayne Gradoz, you two are "Keepers of Hope." You have assisted me in feeling good about myself.

Thank you Julie Hodges for your support; you were the first to call me a "Keeper of Hope," and I won't ever forget it.

Larry Hutto, before the book was even written you had thrown your support behind it, thanks. Thank you to Educational Technology Learning for allowing me the opportunity to spread the message of giving kids hope.

To the faculty and staff of Lee Jr. High and the Central Freshman campus, you are a fantastic group of people to work with.

Bonnie Born, you get a huge "Thank You" for helping me move the book forward financially.

Mark Graham, I truly believe that this book would not have been possible without you. You put the words in my heart onto these pages. It has been fantastic to work with someone that can see through my eyes.

Nick Zelinger, your remarkable book cover design evokes so much emotion; many educators know that child on the cover. Betsy Zelinger, for your special touch. Sue Bray and Bookmasters, you are the greatest people to work with.

Thank you Ed Coyne for your encouragement and my wonderful web site.

To all the kids that have passed through my classroom or office, this book is in honor of you. You have blessed my life more than you will ever know. You have left "Scars of Love" on my soul. Always remember – "I Believe in You."

TABLE OF CONTENTS

PREFACE

PEOPLE OFTEN ASK: *Why Scars of Love?* In response, I tell them this simple story.

Some years ago, on a hot summer day in south Florida, a little boy decided to go for a swim in the heart-shaped lake behind the house he shared with his mother, father, and two sisters. In his haste to cool off, he ran out the back door, leaving behind a trail of shoes, socks, and shirt as he went. He launched himself from the rickety wooden dock and flew into the water, squealing with delight. The boy was a good swimmer, and he propelled himself with ease toward the middle of the lake, completely unaware of the alligator swimming his way.

His mother, as good fortune would have it, was watching her son, as she often did, from the kitchen window of their house. Suddenly she spied the alligator and realized the fearsome creature was headed directly for her son. In utter fear, she ran outside and raced down the path toward the water, yelling to her son as loudly as she could.

Hearing the imploring sound of his mother's voice, the little boy became alarmed. He made a quick U-turn, saw his mom gesturing anxiously, and began swimming toward shore with as much speed as his little arms and legs could muster. He was not fast enough, however. An instant before he reached the dock and his mother's outstretched hand, the alligator opened his powerful jaws. The frantic mother grabbed her little boy's arms at the exact moment the alligator snatched his legs. An incredible tug-of-war ensued. The alligator was much stronger than the mother, but she was far too passionate and determined to ever let go. Love drove her on.

A farmer happened to be driving past at that exact moment and heard her desperate screams. He brought his truck to a screeching halt, snatched his gun, and raced down the path to the lakeshore. He took aim and shot the alligator. The mother pulled her son to shore, and they drove him straight to the hospital.

Remarkably, after weeks and weeks of intensive care and many prayers, the little boy survived. His legs were extremely scarred by the alligator's vicious attack, but his spirit was intact.

Shortly thereafter, a newspaper reporter came to the hospital to interview the boy.

"Will you show me your scars?" he asked.

The boy didn't hesitate. He pushed aside the blanket covering his legs. The reporter gasped. "I've never seen such terrible scars," he exclaimed.

"That's nothing," the boy replied with obvious pride. "Let me show you the scars that really count. These are my best scars."

He rolled up the sleeves of his hospital gown and pointed to the scars on his arms. He said, "Look at these. These are from my mom. She refused to let me go. She wouldn't give up. She wouldn't give up because she loves me, and I have these scars to prove it."

─────────

So every day I ask myself which kind of scars am I leaving? And the answer is the only one I am capable of leaving. As a teacher, woman, and keeper of hope, I choose to leave scars of love on the kids I see every day, not scars of hurt.

INTRODUCTION

~ No Child Will Be Left Behind! ~

IF I, AS an educator, don't believe those six words with all my heart, then the students in my care aren't going to believe them either. I have always lived by these words. And while I might write this book from a teacher's point of view, and while it may in part be written with my fellow teachers in mind, it is meant for anyone who loves kids and longs for their happiness and success.

———

My students call me Sunshine, or Ms. G., or Mama Go, or the Good Morning Lady. My office is open to them every minute of the day. The title next to my door might read "At-Risk Coordinator," but the formality stops the moment they step past the threshold. Inside, I have tried to create an atmosphere that exudes warmth and safety: a place of trust. The first thing a student sees is a bowl of candy sitting on an old credenza. I call it my "squirrel bowl." The theory is to "draw 'em in," the way pecans entice squirrels preparing for a long winter, but really the candy is just another way to make contact, to share a smile, and to let them know I'm available.

Inside the credenza is my collection of willow-tree angels. The angels each have a special meaning. They remind me just how different each child who comes into my office is. They remind me that every student is an individual with individual problems, and that they deserve to be treated as such. Each angel has a message. The angel of healing reminds me that the young girl who comes into my office filled with heartache and feeling beaten down by the world needs healing before she can have her hope restored. The angel of love reminds me that the boy living under a bridge in a broken-down car needs warmth and kindness before he can give his all to math or science. My angels remind me that sometimes I have to let go of what I am seeing with the eyes in my head and trust what the eyes of my heart and soul are telling me instead.

The office has a homey feel to it, and I suppose it reflects my personality. I make sure there are plenty of flowers and books spread around. I've hung a wind chime in the entry and an American flag on the wall. There is a worn, comfortable couch that lets my students know this is a place where they can feel secure. A plaque on the wall says: "Good friends are like angels; you don't have to see them to know they're there."

A stuffed bear – a gift from one of my students – keeps watch over the microwave and holds a sign that reads: *Angel on Duty.* That is quite a compliment.

Another gift was the pencil drawing someone did of me. Beneath the portrait is one of my mantras: "Making a Difference."

The framed needlepoint plaque next to the portrait has four words on it: "Tender Love and Care." That, I suppose, is my other mantra, and I try to live by it every day.

My goal as a teacher is simple and straightforward. My goal is to give every child in my care an honest sense of hope. My goal for this book is to inspire you to see inside every child who enters your life or takes a seat in your classroom. I want to inspire you to leave those children feeling hopeful. If they feel hopeful today, maybe they'll remember the feeling tomorrow. And if they feel hopeful tomorrow, maybe the feeling will last for the rest of their lives. Sometimes this requires only a smile and a friendly greeting. Other times it takes knowing and understanding what it is that makes their world the complicated place that it is.

Sometimes it takes digging deeper and requires time you might not really have. It's not easy when you have 140 kids passing through your classroom every day. But that is, after all, why we became teachers in the first place. It's not easy volunteering a couple of hours a week to mentor a child in need if you're working a full-time job and very likely raising your own family. It's not easy being a "keeper of hope," but that is a role I would encourage every adult to accept and recognize. If we can plant seeds of hope in our children, we can change their lives in a positive way. And if we can do that, then we can call our lives successful.

My kids are called at-risk students because they are more likely to drop-out of school than their peers. Some of them rate with the brightest students in school. Others have serious learning disabilities. Most are somewhere in-between. And then there are those whose intellectual gifts are impossible to judge because the walls they have built around their hearts and souls are nearly impenetrable.

I don't try and detach myself from my kids. I can't. I can't detach myself from their pain. I also know, however, that the very worst thing I can give them is sympathy. Sympathy robs them of hope. It handicaps them. What I give them instead is empathy, because empathy tells them that I understand their pain. It says, "Now let's find a way out of it. Now let me help you build the skills you need to get on with your life."

Kids have to know what they're getting when they come into my office. They have to know that the person they see in the morning, the one who won't let them walk by without a "hello" and a smile, is the same one they are going to encounter when they come to me for a word of advice or a helping hand in the afternoon. If they come to expect a positive attitude, then I have to be consistent. Otherwise, I've lost their trust, and it won't matter how cozy my office is.

I suppose it helps that I am a positive person by nature; I'm one of those people who believe that every day is a good day. Is it important that I keep my private life out of the office? Most of the time it is. My kids don't need to know every detail of my life for me to be effective. There are occasions when sharing a slice of my private life reminds them that I am just as human as they are, and that I also have my struggles. However, most of my kids are totting around a tremendous amount of hard luck, and I try to carry some of that weight for them. I don't enable them. What I do instead is show them I am willing to partner with them in getting beyond their problems, finding solutions, and creating a sense of self-worth and positive momentum.

~ My Personal Wake-Up Call ~

MY WAKE-UP call came early. In fact, it came six weeks into my first year of teaching, in a town so small that one building housed every grade, first through twelfth, and a total of 300 kids.

I was a teacher during the day and a coach once the final bell rang. I did it all: volleyball, tennis, basketball, and track. I even helped with off-season football.

For six weeks, I was one of those teachers who thought education was a matter of perfect attendance, perfect penmanship, and perfect posture. I was so focused on "curriculum" that I couldn't see the individual child. All I saw was a warm body in a seat.

The following poem, which I wrote that first year, describes the turning point in my teaching career. It also marks a change in my teaching philosophy that has sustained me throughout the years. I only wish I had come by it under different circumstances.

16

May I Never Forget

God, she needed someone
And I wasn't there.
How many others have been
Passed by over the years?

There she sat, in the back of the room,
So quiet, just another warm body,
No different from the rest:
Two eyes, a nose, and a mouth.

At lunch, she ate by herself.
Being the first week of school
I let it pass me by:
This loneliness she felt.

Her work was always on time.
She never asked any questions.
Never forgot her book,
And I never paid her any attention.

She never knew her father,
And her mother never cared.
She was an only child,
Lonely and so scared.

I will always remember that day,
The day she didn't come.
She died that morning,
Nothing to hold onto, no will to live.

The empty seat in the back
Is a constant reminder
If only I had taken the time
To share a little love.

Each year, I look at their faces
And wonder if one of them
Is silently begging for
A sense of belonging.

Not one of my students, I pray,
Will ever leave my class
Without having had a little
TENDER LOVE AND CARE!

I changed in the wake of that little girl's death. I was no longer the teacher who did it all by the book. I was no longer the neophyte who thought she had learned all there was to know about education during four years of college. Unfortunately, there is no college course on the art of acknowledging children for who they are. There is no class on validation. We were not taught how to make kids feel good about themselves and their lives. Yes, I remember sitting through classes on discipline management, curriculum, lesson-planning, and classroom control, but there was not one class, seminar, or lecture on how to love the kid sitting in the back row with a troubled heart.

I still get a tear in my eye every time I read that poem. For years I hoped it would stop hitting me so hard. I hoped the emotions evoked by that incident would lessen somewhat, and maybe someday disappear altogether. Now I hope that time never comes. I know that every child who walks into my office or sits in my classroom needs someone to believe in him or her. They need to feel important and wanted. And I never want to forget that again.

~ The Starfish ~

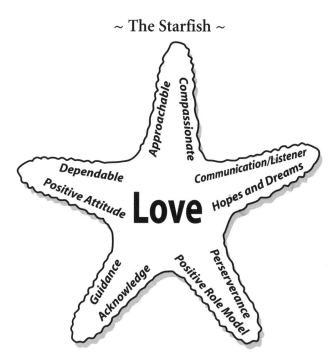

THE STARFISH YOU see here represents what I believe are the many hats that an effective "keeper of hope" must wear. It represents the tools that have helped me to acknowledge and validate my kids, to make them feel good about themselves and their place in the world, and, most importantly by far, to show them how much I care for them as people and individuals, not just as warm bodies. It should be no surprise to find love at the center of this model, because none of the attributes we are going to talk about mean a thing if they don't lead to a willingness to love the kids in our care.

The Starfish Poem

Once upon a time there was a wise man
who used to go to the shore to do his writing.

He had a habit of walking on the beach
before opening his journal and setting to work.

One day, in the distance, he saw someone dancing at the water's edge.
It made him smile to think that the day could provoke
such joyous behavior,
And he began walking faster.

As he came closer, he saw it was a young man.
However, the young man wasn't dancing.
Instead, he was reaching down to the sand,
picking up something, and very gently throwing it into the ocean.

"Good morning!" the sage called. "What are you doing?"

The young man paused, looked up, and replied,
"Throwing starfish in the ocean."

"I guess I should have asked, *why* are you throwing starfish
in the ocean?"

"The sun is up and the tide is going out. If I don't throw them in,
they'll die."

"But, young man, don't you realize that there are miles
and miles of beach and starfish all along it.
You can't possibly make a difference!"

The young man listened politely.
Then he bent down, picked up another starfish,
and threw it past the breaking waves and into the sea.

To the wise man, he said,
"It made a difference for that one."

This young man clearly symbolizes the "keeper of hope" that I
believe exists in each one of us. That is who we are. In the pages that
follow, please allow me to introduce you to the attributes that I feel are
most important in being an effective "keeper of hope."

~ CHAPTER ONE ~

A Keeper of Hope is APPROACHABLE

THE WORD "APPROACHABLE" defines a person who makes herself accessible. She is someone who is easy to meet. She is someone who is easy to know. It's not a bad definition. However, making yourself accessible is not so much a learned skill as it is an attitude.

This is where the foundation of any positive relationship is laid. Kids know in an instant if an adult qualifies as someone they would consider approachable. Teacher, mentor, parent; it doesn't matter. They have to know that the door is open to them, figuratively and literally. The door to your heart has to be open to them, just as the door to your office must be.

~ The Good Morning Lady ~

MY SCHOOL DAY starts the same way every morning. There is a concrete pillar outside the front entrance, and that is where you will find me at 7:15: me, my coffee cup, and my walkie-talkie. That's my perch. As the kids file in, they know Ms. Goforth will be there, checking their I.D. badges, calling out their names, smiling, teasing, and acting a little goofy at times.

"Good morning, Mona. How was your weekend?"

"Hey, Edward. How many more days until Friday?"

"Good morning, Sunshine. Get that I.D. badge on, please."

"Good to see you this morning, Robert. I missed you yesterday."

I freely admit to being a non-stop chatterbox, throwing out positive energy like bait to fish, and taking energy in return from every smile, wave of the hand, or nod of the head. I can't just go through the motions. A positive greeting is part of my job description, the job description I've written for myself.

I never really understood how important those ten minutes in the morning were until I ran into a student and his mother in the grocery store and overheard him say to her, "Hey, that's the Good Morning Lady!"

An early morning greeting is just a beginning, but the kids do take notice. I am acknowledging their existence. I am trying to get their day off on the right foot. But I am also making myself known to them. I am becoming approachable, even if they don't recognize it as such. Whether it's a hug in the hallway, or a question about the dress code, the seeds of a relationship have been sown.

~ The Magic of an Upbeat Attitude ~

A SUCCESSFULLY APPROACHABLE educator has to demonstrate an UPBEAT attitude. It is not always easy, but it is essential. I take it as a challenge to be buoyant and positive with my students even after a day in which I feel I've given everything I can give. Because the moment I see a student respond positively – and sometimes a scowl can be as positive as a smile – I take energy from it.

Me? I'm naturally an upbeat person. Not everyone is. If it doesn't come naturally, it may require a bit of acting. But an upbeat attitude is still necessary if a kid of any age is going to recognize you as someone they can approach with a question or a problem, someone they might come to trust, or someone they might open up to and reveal a small part of their selves.

If I tell a kid, "You know, you're been so good this week that I want you to take Saturday and Sunday off," he or she might look at me like I'm crazy, but they won't forget that I'm here for them, that I'm open, and that I'm approachable.

~ Just Be Glad to See Them ~

TWENTY-SEVEN YEARS ago, I chose to become a teacher. I chose to impart whatever knowledge, wisdom, or insight I could muster to every student who set foot in my classroom every day. It seemed a natural part of my job to be glad to see my students, and it seemed natural to show them that I felt that way. I began every session by telling my kids that I was the luckiest teacher in the world. When they would ask why, I would say, "Because they only give me the most wonderful kids on campus, that's why. I always get the best. And the great thing is, I never have any discipline problems because all my kids are here to learn."

It's as simple as planting a seed. Kids who have been told they're the best will rise to the occasion. On the other hand, kids who have been told they're the most unruly, inattentive students a teacher has ever taught will certainly live up to the billing. That is just the way it works; kids will hold true to whatever expectation a teacher offers.

Twenty-seven years later, I feel exactly the same way. Smiles and greetings are compulsory with me, and the hallway is no different from my office. And the smiles and greetings are genuine, no matter how rough the day has been. They're genuine because sincerity is part of teaching; it's also part of being a human being.

If I'm not excited to see my students file in the door, I should find another profession. Kids deserve the best I can give them. Mediocrity in the classroom is not something I have ever been comfortable with.

Kids are impressionable no matter what their age. They want to be wanted. They want their presence to be meaningful. If I'm genuine in my enthusiasm, they know. And if it's genuine, they respond. In that way, they are no different from you or me. It's just human nature.

It may not be easy for a classroom teacher preparing for seven classes and 140 students every day to give everyone the kind of personal attention that an At-Risk Coordinator like me is able to give. But I made every effort to do so when I was in the classroom, and I know many teachers who do. In any case, every teacher can and should make themselves accessible to their students, whatever the number. I believe we can build a relationship with every student. As teachers, we have to be willing and able to see beyond the curriculum. We have to be willing and able to see beyond the homework and the tardiness.

I had a student in my office recently who had received a zero after missing a homework assignment. The teacher who was so quick with this failing grade had no idea that the boy's family had been evicted from their apartment the night before and had been forced to spend the night in their car under a bridge. He had arrived at school carrying an emotional burden that few of us ever have to face. A homework assignment was far down his list of priorities. He had come to school as much for the warmth and safety of the building as he had for any educational reasons. Who could blame him? And if he were lucky enough to be on the school's free or reduced-cost lunch program, he would actually have something to eat that day.

As teachers, we have to recognize that a student's priorities are not always the same as the ones we walk into the classroom intending to pursue.

Why is a particular student tardy every morning? Are there mitigating circumstances at home? Has his mom been forced to move into a shelter on the far side of town? Is he still trying to figure out where and when the bus will pick him up?

Why is a once-promising girl falling asleep every day in class? Is it possible there's a problem at home that we don't know about? Kids don't offer this information. As teachers, we have to dig deeper.

In this particular situation, I ask the girl's home room teacher if she has tried to contact her parents, and the teacher tells me the phone has been disconnected. I call the student into my office. I offer her a Tootsie Roll from my squirrel bowl. We talk. When the conversation turns to how much she has been sleeping in class, she finally admits that her father has been coming home drunk at night and throwing things. She has spent the last five nights hiding under her bed, too scared to close her eyes. She comes to school where it feels calm and safe by comparison. Calm and safe enough to get some sleep. It took some digging, but the truth is now out in the open, and we as teachers can begin to work with her, not against her.

Kids may not always remember the names of the thirteen colonies or be able to recall the Pythagorean theorem, but they will remember how I made them feel in my class. They may not be able to recite Shakespeare or write code for software, but they will remember if I say, "I missed you yesterday. Class wasn't the same without you." They may not score 100 on a test or be an "A" student in English, but if I tell them I take it personally when they cut class, and that I need them in my classroom, they will feel a sense of validation they may not receive anywhere else.

For me, it's a simple equation; a warm smile and a "good job" go a lot further than a scornful look and a reprimand.

~ A Student's Plea ~

WHAT DOES A child need? Let a child tell you first hand. This is a page from Linda's journal, written in a pre-AP English class. It portrays a student who has fallen between the cracks and provides a disturbing example of how precarious one young lady's life can be.

~ Open Your Ears and See Me ~

Monday: Do you know me? I am a nine-digit number on your attendance form, a smudged box on your seating chart, and the resident in the last chair in the last row.

On the first day of school, I was the last one listed on the class roster. Maybe the paperwork was lost, or perhaps I never returned it. When you asked me for my name, I responded in a tone not much louder than a whisper. Instead of prompting me with a smile, you stood at the front of the room and repeated the question in a raised voice. Did you think I was deaf? Could you have moved a little closer instead of shouting?

You gave us an information sheet on which we were expected to provide you all our personal information. You handed mine back when I was unable to fill in all the blanks. Did you expect me to know the phone number for the prison that my father has called home for the last ten years? He has been there since that fateful day when the policeman came to my school and asked me all those questions about his behavior toward me.

What address should I put for the last parking space in the abandoned lot across from the factory? That's the place we have called home since we were thrown out of our apartment. The landlord didn't seem to understand or care that a family of five can't survive on the $320 we receive from the government each month.

Thursday: Today, for the first time since school began, I failed to complete a homework assignment. You questioned my understanding of your expectations. Would it have made any difference if I had told you that I had spent all night in the emergency room at the hospital hoping and praying that my little brother's appendicitis had been treated in time?

Friday: You gave me an extra day to complete my assignment, but the second night was spent sitting in the parking lot with my siblings waiting for my mom to return from my brother's bedside. This time you questioned my desire. "Do you want to repeat this course in summer school?" you asked. Since that day, you no longer seem to notice whether or not my paper is completed.

Tuesday: After I had been absent for a week, you stopped me in the hall. You were sympathetic and wanted to know what was going on. Was I all right? I really wanted to share the burden I had been carrying around, but the bell rang and your concern seemed to disappear. Suddenly you were more interested in directing me into the room and toward my desk so that class could start on time. Were you really concerned, or was it just background information for your teacher discussions in the lounge later that day? You may as well know. My mom left us with her friend while she climbed on the back of a motorcycle driven by some man she had met at a bar the night before. She came back a week later with a black eye and bruises that she couldn't or wouldn't explain.

Friday: When I sat through class with my head on my desk, you came by and tapped me on the shoulder. I returned to that position a few minutes later, but you didn't even bother to try again. Did you realize that perhaps getting some much-needed rest was more important than the day's lesson? Yes, on that particular day, I did need some rest. After school, I work for my grandmother and my aunt cleaning offices to help my mom with our expenses. On that particular day, I had worked until midnight because my grandmother was sick and couldn't help us.

Monday: You were nice enough when the other kids started making off-handed remarks about my appearance. It didn't stop the taunting, but at least they didn't say those things in your classroom. It's really difficult to appear chic when your closet is the trunk of a car. Using cheap perfume to cover the smell of old motor oil and gasoline is pretty futile.

Tuesday: You turned in my name to the school service worker when my grades dropped below passing and my absences rose to double digits. After a half-dozen unsuccessful attempts at contacting my mom, the service worker turned my case over to Child Protection Services. When the CPS investigator came around asking questions, Mom started to worry that they would take us away from her and decided it was time to hit the road. She packed what belongings we have into the back of our old, decrepit car. Her plan is to drive until the car breaks down, or we run out of gas money.

So as you read this journal – if you read this journal – I am sandwiched in the back of our car headed for some unknown destination with my worn-out mom and a pack of dirty, hungry children. I write these words knowing that I may never again sit in a classroom as a student. When we stop this dilapidated roller coaster that we're on, I plan to find a job and somebody to marry so that I can take care of my sister and brothers.

Please don't blame yourself. I don't blame you. You have a job that doesn't allow you time for students like me. I have turned out better than a lot of others. If things had been different, maybe I could have gone to college and been something remarkable. Things didn't turn out that way, and so we will never know what could have been.

In a few days, a new student will check into your class bringing a new nine-digit number, filling the smudged box on the chart, and occupying "my" seat in the last chair of the last row. Will you raise your voice when he mumbles, or question his understanding or desire? Will you pretend to be sympathetic or just give up after a while? He will be my brother, treat him well. Open your eyes and see him. Open your ears and hear him. Open your heart and know him. Open your mind and care for him. Linda.

~ Mona's Story ~

NINTH-GRADERS ARE, in many ways, the ultimate contradiction. They can be tough, indulgent, and selfish. They can be scared and uncertain. They can be unreadable and inscrutable. And yet their age is so demanding and so confusing, as they walk the line between adolescence and adulthood, innocence and overload, laughter and tears, that their emotions are often tethered by a thread.

When I see tears, the way I did when Mona and her mother were walking toward me in the hall that day, I don't worry about being subtle or stepping on people's toes. I jump in with both feet.

I intercepted them with a smile and a wave. Mona was as short as her mother was tall, but both had beautiful, expressive faces. Mona's face was streaked with tears, and she was shaking like a leaf.

"Hi, I'm Ms. Goforth," I said to her mother. "Is everything okay, ma'am?"

She shook her head. "We have a problem at home," she admitted. "A domestic violence issue."

"Okay. Well, let's go down to my office and sort things out." I led them down the hall. "When did it happen? This morning?"

"No, ma'am. Last night. Mona's grandfather tried to attack us with a butcher knife."

"Okay," I said calmly. I may have been appalled and outraged, but expressing that was not what Mona and her mother needed right then.

"Let's talk to one of our counselors and see what we can do. Have the police been notified?"

"Yes, ma'am. They came to the house last night. Mona was the one who called 911. She was the last one out of the house."

"It must have been terrifying."

I took them to the counselor's office and requested the presence of the police officer on duty that day. Mona's grandfather, I discovered, had spent the night in jail. A domestic disturbance charge had been filed. Her grandmother had gotten a restraining order. When information about the knife and the attack were revealed to the police, they filed an assault with a deadly weapon charge, placing the grandfather behind bars for three months. This was good news, but it wasn't enough to stop Mona from shaking.

"Don't worry, darlin'," I said to her. "No one is going to hurt you now. They'll have to get through me first."

Mona hadn't slept a wink after the attack. She was as exhausted as she was frightened. Unfortunately her mother was expected at work, and Mona wouldn't let go of her hand. She couldn't go home, and she didn't want to be in class, so I offered her the couch in my office.

The on-duty police officer also assured Mona that she was safe, but no amount of reassurance could erase the image of a drunken grandfather stalking her with a butcher knife. She would live with that image forever, and all I could do was wrap my arms around her and let her cry and shake. She kept talking about the "look on her granddad's face."

Another piece of trust had been stolen from Mona. Maybe I could restore a little slice of that trust here in my office.

I let her sleep. Then I had some of her class work delivered to my office. After an hour, she said, "I'd like to go back to class now, Ms. Goforth."

This was an encouraging sign. I wasn't urging her to return to class; this was Mona's decision. She felt safe enough and secure enough to re-enter the world of her fellow students, and this was monumental.

"If you get spooked," I told her, "You come right back down to my office."

This was only the beginning. I received a subpoena to appear at trial, and Mona was also scheduled to testify. The charges included attempted murder, because the grandfather had used the grandmother's name when he said, "I'm going to kill you."

The good news was that we were sequestered together, so Mona had someone to talk to. She was terrified by the thought of taking the witness stand and looking down at her grandfather's face. "What do I do, Ms. Goforth? I'm so scared."

"All you have to do, Mona, is tell the truth," I said. "Just tell them exactly what happened."

Mona took the stand and told her side of the story. Then she endured the relentless attacks of the defense until she finally broke down in tears. When she returned to the waiting room, sobbing and crying, she kept asking me why the defense attorney had been so mean to her. I didn't know what to say.

The case against the grandfather fell apart when Mona's grandmother took the stand and swore that none of it had happened.

As appalling and sobering as this was, the story ended well, or at least as well as it could. Mona and her mother packed their bags and moved as far away from San Angelo as their car would take them. Will Mona ever be able to sleep again without reliving the nightmare of that evening? I can only hope so.

It was, nonetheless, a crisis averted. I had seen Mona's tears, and she had recognized me as an advocate when I approached her that day in the hall. We had never spoken previously, but she knew my name.

Maybe she had seen me in the morning or walking through the halls with a smile on my face.

What is important is that she saw me as approachable: approachable enough for her to trust me, to feel safe enough to come into my office, and to feel comfortable enough to tell me her fears.

~ What You See is *Not* Always What You Get ~

AS AN EDUCATOR, I can't qualify my approachability based upon appearance or behavior or reputation. I have to be as receptive to the boy with the Mohawk, nose ring, and ear gauges as I am to the girl with the tattoo, tongue ring, and the snarl. I may not particularly like his Mohawk, or the tattoo she is so proud of, but the body art and the haircut are only the window dressing. It's the child inside I have to see. My smile has to be directed to the girl hiding behind the snarl.

I have to see into their hearts and into their souls. That is my challenge, but it is also the challenge of every adult. What are their gifts? What do they have right now to be grateful for? What are their dreams? What are their strengths? How can I help them achieve those dreams and make the most of their strengths? I can't do that if I'm judging them based on their hairstyle or skin color, their posture or their slang.

For me, the beauty of any child lies within.

A student of mine named Edward once paid me the highest compliment when he said, "Ms. Goforth, all you see is the kid. It doesn't matter if we wear brand-name clothes or not, you just see us."

I've come to realize that being approachable is not a selective state of mind. I can't be approachable on Monday and then close myself off on Friday. If children see me as approachable, they are going to come to me with positive things as well as negative things. I have to be open to both. They are going to come to me with big problems and little problems, and one is no more or no less important to them. They may approach me because they have what seems to be an insurmountable crisis, but they may also drop by my office just because they need someone to connect with them.

I try very hard to give every issue equal weight. I try very hard to see every issue as important.

Some weeks ago, a little girl rushed into my office, all smiles and jubilation, and announced to me, "I'm so excited! We got electricity!"

While there was an undercurrent of sadness knowing that she and her family had actually been going without electricity, this was a moment of celebration for her, and I had to celebrate with her. We hugged and laughed and cheered.

To be receptive without judging is easy when your concern is the human being standing in front of you and not how they look in the eyes of society. It's easy when you're willing to be open and approachable. The reward is trust. And when a child trusts you, suddenly the possibility of planting seeds of hope becomes a reality.

~ CHAPTER TWO ~

A Keeper of Hope is COMPASSIONATE

COMPASSION, AS I see it, does not relate to the classic definition that suggests "deep sympathy for another's misfortune." The compassion that a teacher shows toward a student or that a mentor demonstrates toward a young man or woman has more to do with understanding and listening. It has more to do with our ability as adults in truly seeing a situation through the eyes of the kids with whom we are trying to work.

If one of my students approaches me with a problem or a concern, or simply with the need to vent, I can't do them any good if I am looking at their situation from my own personal view of the world. I have to turn the tables and look through their eyes.

I don't react, even when they are relating a story that is tearing me up inside or sending shivers of anguish up my spine, and some of their stories are that powerful.

Over-reacting is a curse. There are only two consequences to over-reacting, and neither is healthy or helpful. If a students thinks: "Wow, I'm really getting to her," it can lead to an embellishment of the facts or even out-in-out fabrication. The student is no longer seeking a solution to a real problem. Now he or she is feeding off the energy of a work of fiction.

Over-reacting can also have the opposite effect, as well. The student may read my reaction as a condemnation of the situation. If he or she perceives my reaction as a judgment about their behavior, the most common defense mechanism is to clam up completely, and go into a shell until they're dismissed. What this silence is saying in effect is, "I've done something wrong. I'm a bad person." Once they begin thinking along those lines, it's a hard hole to dig out of, and I am no longer an ally. I am no longer someone they can trust. And regaining the trust of a 15-year-old is nearly impossible.

It is far more effective to demonstrate compassion for their plight by acknowledging their right to feel exactly the way they do and by validating the situation as real and important.

Pity is the last thing any of us want. My students are no different in that regard than I am. When I suffered a series of strokes in the fall of 2000, the last thing I wanted to hear was, "Oh, Debbie, bless your heart, you poor thing." Thanks, but no thanks.

Yes, I may have had a difficult time writing for a while, and it may have taken several months before I regained full function of my left leg. I wanted friends and family to understand my struggles, but I didn't want them to feel sorry for me. I intended to rise up again and push forward with my life, and nothing was going to keep me down.

Most of the children who approach me in the hall with a question or a problem or come into my office for a Tootsie Roll and a word of counsel are looking at life with this same mindset: understand me, hear me, support me. But please don't pity me.

Sympathy is debilitating. It steals your fire.

Empathy is empowering. It sends a message of hope.

When I returned to school after my strokes, limping down the hall like a woman in slow motion, I was greeted by two kinds of people. The pain of seeing me like this was so great and so embarrassing for some people that they would avoid me at all cost, finding some convenient excuse for ducking back into their classrooms or turning the other direction. Then there was the group who made eye contact, pumped their fists, and said, "Atta girl, Debbie. You're looking good. Keep it up. One day at a time."

The first group meant me no harm, but their sympathy also did me no good. The second acknowledged the fight I was waging. They were not overwhelmed by it. This gave me strength and courage. It also gave me hope.

That is the true nature of compassion. Compassion empowers. Compassion is a sharing of strength, courage, and hope.

~ Rejection Hurts From the Inside Out ~

RAMON WAS AN early victim of my squirrel bowl and the Tootsie Rolls I use to entice kids into my office, if only to say "Hello," if only to let them know that I am there if they need anything: advice, counsel, a place to vent, or a shoulder to cry on.

Ramon was an example of how sometimes I have to bring the squirrel bowl to them before they'll come to the squirrel bowl in the office.

This is trickier than it sounds. While I can almost always spot the kids who are headed for trouble – by the way they carry themselves, by the look in their eyes by the company they keep – it is not always easy to reach them.

I make a habit of keeping my pockets filled with Tootsie Rolls. When I see a group of kids huddled together on the campus grounds or in the cafeteria, I don't hesitate to walk their way and plunge right in. This is the tricky part, because I have now entered their circle. I have crossed into their territory. So the most I can do is say, "Hello, how's it going?" I don't push. I'm just trying to open the door to a relationship. I pass out a few pieces of candy and say, "If you ever want to come by the office, the door is always open. So is the squirrel bowl."

Once they're in my office, the rules change. They are now in my space, my territory, and I can be more open and forthright.

That's how it began with Ramon. A foray into his circle led to a visit into mine. Like so many others, Ramon didn't realize at the time that dropping by my office for a piece of candy was the first step in building our relationship.

Ramon was a special education student. His behavior was typical of many kids who struggle in the classroom. Instead of asking for help, which they see as an admission of academic failings, they lash out, preferring the reputation of an angry, hard-headed kid as opposed to a dumb one. Ramon had been known for acting-out in class, swearing at anyone who posed a threat – including teachers – and periodically kicking a wastebasket. Better to suffer the disciplinary consequences than to ask for help.

I had seen lots of kids like Ramon. Someone had called them stupid along the way, or a "special ed," and from that day forward they were driven by insecurity, and insecurity almost always leads to behavioral issues.

After Ramon had been kicked out of the credit recovery lab and more than one of his classes, I "invited" him into my office. Before we could deal with his discipline problems or behavior issues – never an effective first step – I wanted to get to know the Ramon who had spent most of his waking hours trying to survive outside the walls of our school. What did he like to do for fun? Where did he go? Who were his friends? Who did he call family?

For the first fifteen minutes, I talked, and Ramon stared at his hands. It wasn't until the subject of his mother and father came up that Ramon showed any sign of engaging me in mutual conversation.

He didn't say much, but I was able to learn that Ramon was six when his parents shipped him and his brother off to live with his grandparents. His brother was four at the time. Ramon didn't have an explanation for this decision, but he had spent enough time thinking about it to evolve a theory: either his parents couldn't afford to raise two toddlers, or they didn't want them. Good guesses.

The boys lived with their grandparents for six years. When Ramon talked about his grandmother, the love he felt for her was obvious, like an open book. When I saw the glint of a tear in his eyes, I knew I had him; I knew this was the road I needed to lead him down, as painful as it might be. This was the way to his heart.

"What happened in the 6th grade?" I asked him.

"My grandma died."

"I'm sorry. That must have been so hard." I knew there was more to the story, however, and I had to go there with him. I said, "So then what happened? Did you and your brother continue to live with your grandfather?"

Ramon shook his head. "He married some other woman. They moved away and took my little brother. My granddad said, 'I can't take you.'"

The pain of this rejection – the second in his very short life – was like a mask contorting Ramon's normally serene face. I wanted to take him in my arms and save him from the pain, but that was not the answer. Not yet. I said, "Where are you living now, Ramon?"

"With my aunt."

I knew this wasn't true. I knew he was living with different families in the neighborhood and very deep into the gang scene. That wasn't an issue I could deal with at that moment, but I had to take Ramon further down the path. I had to aim for the heart.

"I'm about to do something to you that's going to hurt, Ramon," I said. "I want to tell you that ahead of time, okay?"

He didn't have to say, "What are you talking about?" It was written all over his face.

"You loved your grandmother very much, didn't you, Ramon?"

It was like a dike breaking, the way the tears suddenly appeared in his eyes and spilled out. They coursed down his cheeks and onto his shirt. His shoulders shook, and emotions he had been keeping at bay for years washed over him.

"Yeah, I did," he said, between sobs. "And she loved me so much. We went everywhere with her. We did everything together."

"You miss her, don't you?"

"Yeah. I miss her so much."

"You know that she's watching down on you, don't you? She is, Ramon. And you're going to make her proud. I know you are."

"I want to," he answered.

"And I'll help you," I promised.

We talked and cried and shared, the way confidants do. I told Ramon how important my father and mother had been in my life and how they had helped to shape and mold me into the person I was today. "You haven't had that foundation. But you did have your grandmother."

Ramon wasn't ready to go back to class yet, so we came up with a compromise: a one-page writing assignment designed to work on his intuitive skills. "I want you to think about what makes the perfect parents, Ramon. What would they do? What would they say? How would they treat you? Whatever you think. And then write it down."

Ramon shook his head. "But I can't write. I can't spell."

"I'm not worried about that, Ramon. I'm not grading you on spelling or punctuation. I just want to know what you think would make the perfect parent."

"That's all?"

"That's all."

Ramon took the paper into the office next door. Thirty minutes later, he emerged again and handed me his assignment. I read the words out loud.

"The perfect parent goes outside and plays football with me." Ramon was not an athlete. He was a rough-and-tumble kid who had never participated in sports. But a father or mother who would take the time to toss a ball around with him symbolized something so basic that he had put it at the top of his list.

"A parent that takes care of me and my little brother." Just be responsible; just be there when the chips were down.

"A parent who doesn't do drugs. A parent who loves me and my little brother. A parent who has finished school. A parent who has a job and can put food on the table. And a parent who will spend the summer with me."

Right then, I wanted to cry with Ramon. I wanted to hug him. I wanted to say something profound. But this was one of those times when a reaction would have sent the wrong message. Instead, I looked at the work he had done and said, "You did a great job on your assignment, Ramon. Those are really wonderful things you mentioned. And I want you to strive to be the person you described here, okay? Be this person. Is it a deal?"

"Yeah, it's a deal."

"So this is what I'm going to do. I'm going to keep this paper until the end of the year, and then I'm going to give it back to you. We'll read it over again, and then you can keep it. Then, when the time is right, you can set a goal for yourself of becoming the same wonderful parent you described here."

The bell rang just then, and Ramon returned to class. When the door closed, I sat at my desk and stared down at the simple words Ramon had written. So simple. Just love me. Just put food on the table. Don't do drugs. Was that too much to ask?

After a few tears, I got down to business. Ramon needed a full-time tutor, and the tutor had to be someone who could connect with Ramon and draw him out; had to be someone like his grandmother. It was no coincidence that the woman I chose was a retired schoolteacher with four grandkids.

Ramon's tutor now sits with him in every ALS lab class, and they work together on every assignment. He has blossomed. His grades are improving, and he doesn't act up in class. He's found two people he can call on for help: his tutor, and his campus mom. He has found two people who care, and, most importantly, he has begun to care in return.

~ Onions~

KIDS ARE LIKE onions.

Some have more protective layers to peel away than others. But if I take my time and work my way slowly through the layers, I believe I can reach them. And if I can reach them, then hopefully I can make a difference.

I often start a conversation with a child by asking him or her to list five good things about themselves. Not 10 or 20 or 100, just five. You would be amazed and saddened to know how many of them don't have an answer. It almost brings me to tears thinking about how many of these wonderful kids cannot find even one good thing to say about themselves. Not one. It's more than sad; it's disheartening. I ask myself what drives them? I ask myself what gets them up in the morning and compels them to get dressed and out the door? If they can't give me an answer, then it's my job to find out. It's my job to peel away the layers of that onion, to explore what makes each of them tick, and to expose their hearts and touch their souls.

Ramon's tears were a show of emotion I desperately needed to tap if I was going to get to the root of his problem.

As harsh as it may sound, I know that if I can bring out the tears, the boy or girl sitting across from me is still within my reach. I know then that his or her heart has not been so completely hardened by the blows that life has dealt them that I can't help. I know then that I can still give them a slice of hope.

In Ramon's case, the key was the love and passion he had felt for his grandmother. Crying for her was not a bad thing. It was a healthy show of emotion. It signaled a fork in the road; all I had to do was lead him in the right direction and hope he followed.

I can't reach them all. I know that. That's reality. It doesn't stop me from trying.

~ A Road Map to Success ~

FAILURE IS SELF-PERPETUATING. It's an endless roller coaster many of the kids I see every day have been riding for most of their lives.

It begins with a negative self-image. So many of my kids feel worthless or unimportant or hopeless. Who knows what triggered it in the past? Someone with influence may have said the wrong thing at the wrong time. Maybe they figured out that society rewards position and power and performance.

Many have grown up with drugs, poverty, and failure. They see it everywhere they turn. They're not encouraged to do well because they're too busy just surviving. They look around at the world, and what they see doesn't necessarily make them feel good about who they are and what they have.

This doesn't excuse bad behavior, but it does explain it. We live in a society that deals with bad behavior by doling out various types of punishment. It may be a slap on the wrist, or it may be jail time. While punishment may act as a deterrent to some degree, most of my kids take it as further proof of their second-class status. They either give up or strike back. For many of these kids, the only defense mechanisms they know are anger, violence, and indignation.

It's a downward spiral. I have found only one effective means of rewriting this road map or changing the course of this perpetual roller coaster. I have to target their negative self-image. I have to peel away the layers of their protective onion and expose their hearts. If I can make them believe in themselves, then I can offer them a slice of hope. Hope leads to dreams.

The upside is that most kids have tremendous potential. Most kids have love in their hearts. Most of them want to like the person they see in the mirror every morning. All we have to do is give them a reason.

~ Patty ~

PATTY'S STORY MAY sound simplistic on the surface. It may sound like any 15-year-old acting-out. But Patty was anything but simple, and, in that way, she represents most of the young men and women I meet. Do not underestimate them; that's one of my rules. Don't ever discount their potential; that's another one.

Patty had model good looks and glorious, flowing hair, but she didn't flaunt them. She could scrap with the best of them. That, it appeared, was how she stayed even with the world. Scrap, claw, fight. Never give an inch. Patty would show up at school looking like an alley cat after a very contentious night. Bruised from head to foot. Scratches across her face. Fingernails broken. She would apparently fight anyone. In fact, she probably went looking for fights. But looks can be deceiving.

Patty had been in a downward spiral for three or four months. She was not the same girl who had started classes in September, and I was concerned for her. Very concerned.

Patty attended my credit recovery lab and was on the verge of failing every class. On the surface, she might best be described as self-destructive. I believed differently.

One particular day, Patty was caught using her cell phone in class. This is strictly forbidden. When Patty refused to relinquish her cell phone to the vice-principal, an unpleasant confrontation erupted. By the time I became involved in the situation, Patty was in the office awaiting the arrival of the campus police. With the vice-principal's permission, I decided to intervene.

I knew something of Patty's history, so I wasn't ill-prepared. Her mother was not her most supportive advocate. Her mother had recently invited her boyfriend to take up residence at their house, and the friction between Patty and the boyfriend was explosive. I knew that Patty saw a reflection of the boyfriend in the vice-principal (it could have been any male), and she was not going to back down. Maybe I could help.

I invited her out to the common area, and we sat at one of the picnic tables listening to the first birds of spring chirping. I said, "You know, Patty, I don't think you came to school in September planning to fail every class. I just don't see you as that kind of girl. You've got too much spunk and too many brains. Something happened several months ago that changed things, and I sure would like to know what it was. Would you like to tell me?"

"I had a rough time," she answered.

"What happened, sweetheart? You can tell me."

"I miscarried," she said painfully.

"I'm sorry. How far along were you?"

"Four months."

"Have you shared this with anyone, Patty?"

"I told my mom. She said I deserved it," she said. "I guess I'm just not a very good person."

I could feel my blood boil, but I also realized that over-reacting would not be in Patty's best interest. Instead I told her, "First of all, no one deserves to go through a miscarriage. Maybe your mom feels you can be more responsible when it comes to the choices you make, which is fine, but no one *deserves* to go through what you did. The second thing is, you're not a bad person. In fact, you're an amazing young lady. Never forget that. Okay?"

She smiled. "Yes, ma'am." But then the smile disappeared. "She wants me to move out of the apartment so she can keep her boyfriend." As disturbing as this dynamic sounded, me judging her mother was not in Patty's best interest. "That doesn't feel very good, does it?"

She shook her head. "I used to live with my grandma, and it was great. She was the only one who ever really cared for me. But she moved away because she and my dad don't get along."

There was a thread of hope running through this, and I wanted to cultivate it. "Do you stay in touch with your grandma?" I asked. "Do you talk on the phone or exchange letters?"

Patty stared at the floor. "No, I haven't. I don't know her new address, and she doesn't know that I live with my mom."

"Why don't you do that? Why don't you see if you can get your grandma's address and write to her?"

Patty perked up. We talked a few more minutes about the idea before I said, "But we still have a problem. You've dug yourself a hole. You were rude to the vice-principal. Now you have a choice. You're probably going to be sent to Carver (the alternative school) for a while, but what we can do is go back in there and stop digging the hole." She knew what I meant. "I know you don't want to give the vice-principal your phone, but will you?"

After a long and tortured hesitation, she said, "Yeah, I guess."

We went back inside and met with the vice-principal. I said, "I just want you to know that Patty's going through a tough time right now." I didn't go into the details, and he didn't ask me to elaborate. Patty reluctantly gave up her cell phone, but I couldn't ask her to apologize. I never do that. In essence, that is much the same as me apologizing on the student's behalf, and no one benefits. Instead I said, "Is there anything else you'd like to say, Patty?"

The question phrased as such generally accomplishes the desired result, and it did so in Patty's case. She said, "I'm sorry. I was just having a bad day."

In the end, the vice-principal decided against sending Patty to the alternative school. We dealt with the problem in-house.

Patty's is a positive story. She turned things around in school. She did write that letter to her grandmother, and her grandmother invited her for a visit. The visit turned into a permanent living situation, and Patty is well on her way to graduating from high school.

~ Holding a Grudge ~

HERE IS A last thought regarding the struggles of maintaining a compassionate approach toward the young men and women we encounter every day. Kids say and do things that hurt, and sometimes it's not easy putting those things aside. But I've discovered that holding a grudge against a student is as damaging to the process as over-reacting. Several years back, Judy, a student not unlike Patty in her aggressive tendencies, called me a name best left to the imagination. I said, "Oh, my goodness," and invited her to accompany me to the office. When her three-day suspension was over, she came back to class, and the first thing I said was, "Welcome back, Judy. We've missed you. Class hasn't been the same without you."

She sat down, and we went back to work. One chapter closed, and another one opened.

~ CHAPTER THREE ~

A Keeper of Hope LISTENS and COMMUNICATES

NORMALLY KIDS DON'T come into my office or stop me in the hall expecting me to solve their problems. More often than not, they just need to vent. Like most of us, they just need someone who is willing to listen. They need someone who will empathize with the rough times they're experiencing. Who doesn't?

Survival can be a lonely business. Trusting another person enough to share the pain and the frustration of daily living is a gift. It doesn't matter what your station in life is or what your financial standing happens to be. But adolescence has its own special problems. Poverty amplifies these problems. Splintered and dysfunctional families, drug abuse, and alcoholism all add fuel to the fire.

But "at-risk" is not a term governed by socio-economic boundaries. I have almost as many kids from affluent homes as I do from poverty-stricken families.

I often see my kids as little bowls brimming with the sorrow, hurt, and anger of their lives. When the struggles seem insurmountable, the cup overflows or collapses. The sorrow, hurt, and anger have to go somewhere, and the results are not always pretty. This is when a teacher refers these wonderful children to me. This is when I send a pass to the child's classroom requesting an audience in my office. I keep it private. There is no big announcement. Some kids look at a visit to my office as an embarrassment, and I will do anything in my power to avoid causing that.

When their hearts are overflowing with turmoil, my office is a place where they can come to yell, cry, or stomp their feet: a place to diffuse some of the pressure, and to know the world isn't going to come to an end in the process.

I let them vent. I listen. I empathize. I don't rush to solve their problems. If a boy's mother or father is abusing drugs at home and falling further into the abyss of addiction, I can't change that. If a young girl's maternal grandmother has been diagnosed with cancer and given six weeks to live, I have no control over that. All I can do is let them flush their systems of the turmoil, and then try and help them summon the strength and courage to face the problem head-on. I can acknowledge their pain and validate their right to feel exactly as they do, and then I can give them as many tools as possible to face life in as positive a light as their unwavering spirits will allow.

They are not looking for a problem-solver as much as an ally. I can be that for them.

I am often surprised at how few allies these young men and women have. If you don't have a family that cares, or have one that's seemingly too busy, and if your friends are trying to keep their heads above water just like you are, bona fide allies are hard to find. A world of drugs, gangs, and insincerity is sometimes all they have, and trust is hard to come by. If I can convince them that my office is a safe, predictable haven, then a trusting relationship is possible.

~ Survival Mode ~

IN MY ROLE as an At-Risk Coordinator, I communicate with teachers at the Central Freshman campus on a regular basis regarding my kids. One of the most common and understandable complaints that I hear is that a child's academic performance is suffering. It's most often not from a lack of intelligence; most often it's a simple case of not caring. In most cases, I tell them that the problem may be more than a simple case of indifference or complacency. It may be a matter of priorities.

"He's in survival mode," I often say. Or, "She's just trying to stay afloat at the moment. Please try and understand."

For some kids, performance at school is a distant second to simply making it to school. On days like that, school is a place to stay warm, eat lunch, and escape the neighborhood. I've seen dozens of kids arrive at school on a 32-degree day with no socks, much less a coat, and wearing a sleeveless shirt and flip-flops. Often times the problem is not a matter of forgetfulness or a lack of planning. The problem is that they don't own a coat, nor do they have clean socks. The problem is survival, our most basic instinct.

If a teacher says to me, "Why didn't he (or she) tell me?" I often say, "Why didn't you ask?"

Kids have pride, just like you and I. They are not going to shout from the rooftops about the deficiencies in their wardrobes.

The answer is to provide the basic necessities so they can start acquiring tools and skills meant to improve their lot in life, like an education. One of the steps I have taken over the years is to create relationships with organizations willing and able to provide some of the bear essentials, like coats or hats. There are so many caring people and dedicated groups that want to help. Many of them just don't know who to talk to or where to go. So I tell them.

Unfortunately, that only serves to highlight the problem, it doesn't cure it.

~ I Just Want to Be a Kid ~

JOEY WAS ON a collision course with jail and the prospect of repeating the 9th grade when he first came to me. He was failing almost every class. The courts had mandated his attendance at school, which meant he was on a very short leash. High school was looking more and more remote.

I called him in. He eased his lanky frame into the chair across from me. He wore jeans and a shirt that looked as if they had been handed down to him by a man twice his size. I wondered when he had last showered.

He looked lost, detached, and anxious. He tapped his foot unconsciously. If ever there was a cup overflowing with pain and anguish, and on the verge of cracking open, this was it. If I could just siphon off a part of that burden!

Step one: break the ice. Get to know him. Open lines of communication. Find something to get him talking, and then be willing to listen.

As it turned out, Joey didn't take much wooing. A warm smile, a Tootsie Roll, a couple of leading questions, and the floodgates opened. He talked about everything: family, friends, school, the streets, survival. I had never seen a boy so eager to unburden himself.

His dad was in prison and would be for a very long time.

Back when they lived in Dallas, his older brother had taken a baseball bat to some guy's head in an argument over drugs and cracked it open "like a ripe melon." Joey had witnessed the incident from start to finish.

He had also witnessed an execution-style slaying in Dallas that he described almost matter-of-factly. "Guy's head was blown clean off," he said. Another drug-related incident.

He had seen another man nearly bleed to death from a knife wound.

He had experienced domestic violence at its worst.

He had served time in jail. He had been arrested and harassed more times than he could count.

He had experimented with drugs, hung with the gangs, and been in dozens of fights.

Listening to Joey, you would have thought you were hearing the glorified tales of a middle-aged man, not the everyday life of a 15-year-old boy. When he had spent the last of his words, he looked across at me with the saddest, most pragmatic eyes in the world and said, "You know, Ms. Goforth, I just want to be a kid. I don't want to see all that stuff and do all these things. I just want to be a kid."

I listened, half in wonder and half in horror. Where would I be if had experienced even half of what Joey had in his short life? Probably in a padded cell somewhere. All he wanted was a chance to be fifteen.

~ I'm Your New Best Friend ~

MARY WAS 14 when I saw her walk onto campus her first day. She was a wisp of a girl with a long, brown ponytail, Capri pants, and a sickly pallor.

She was pregnant – you couldn't miss that, not with her petite frame – and she walked with a painful gait. I could see she was having trouble keeping up with the mad rush of 750 students headed for the entrance, and my first thought was that this poor girl was about to be crushed.

57

I reached out, took her by the arm, and steered her out of harm's way. I said, "Good morning. I'm Ms. Goforth. I'm your new best friend."

She smiled, but it wasn't a trusting smile. The first thing a 14-year-old pregnant girl expects is some rebuke for her obvious predicament. I had to show her that not everyone viewed her that way.

"What's your name? You do have a name, don't you?" I teased.

"Mary."

"That's a beautiful name, Mary." I ushered her inside. "Come with me."

I led her into my office. She stopped in front of the plaque that said: "Good friends are like angels; you don't have to see them to know they're there."

"This is your safe haven," I told her. "Any time you need something, you're coming here. Okay?"

Mary would be in my office many times over the next few months, and I would become, in many ways, her surrogate mother. Her track record with meaningful relationships was not good, and she was starved for someone to fill the void. The father of her baby had skipped town the minute he heard she was pregnant. Her own father had died of a drug overdose when she was twelve. Her mother was in and out of jail. To say that Mary was lacking positive role models was a sad understatement.

She lived with her grandmother. Outside of school, the one and only person Mary could rely on was her 20-year-old half-brother, Benjamin. Every day, Benjamin delivered Mary to and from school and then went off to work a full day at a construction job. Mary didn't have many angels in her life, but Benjamin was certainly one.

The more pregnant Mary became, the more problematic her juvenile arthritis became. Her spindly legs ached most of the time, and Mary didn't have a primary care physician with whom to consult. When things got too bad, she visited the emergency room of the hospital. The doctors told her that as long as she was pregnant, they couldn't prescribe arthritis medicine. Instead, they recommended Ibuprofen and the possibility of homebound schooling until the baby arrived. Mary returned to school with a bottle of Ibuprofen, but she still arrived every morning with tears in her eyes because the pain was so severe.

I had seen enough. I stepped out of the box and called her doctor. Mary's OB told me that I was the first adult other than Benjamin who had shown even the slightest interest in Mary's condition. This little wisp of a girl had gone to every appointment alone. Fortunately the OB recommended Mary to a primary care physician who agreed to see her and accept her mother's Medicaid for payment. I set up the appointment, and Benjamin drove her.

I was in my office when the phone rang.

"Ms. Goforth. It's Mary. Would you do me a favor and talk to the doctor for me?" Mary didn't have to say that she didn't have anyone else to turn to. "Could you listen to what he's saying and then explain it to me later?"

It was worth everything we had been through to know she trusted me enough to call, and I said, "You betcha."

This new primary care doctor didn't want Mary to be homebound schooled. He thought it was in Mary's best interest to stay active and mobile. "But I am warning you," he said, "Mary is going to have some good days and some real bad days. And the only medicine I want her taking is Ibuprofen."

As Mary grew closer to full-term, I told her she could start taking the elevator to her second-floor classes, and that I would provide her with an elevator key. She refused. She wanted to climb the stairs like everyone else. Every day I would see her reading her baby books and preparing for motherhood. Some days she would come into my office so wracked with pain that I would lead her to my couch, cover her with a blanket, and say, "Hang on, Mary. Forty-five minutes." By then, we knew exactly how long it took for the Ibuprofen to kick in.

The next day she would arrive at school with the most radiant smile. "Good day?" I asked.

"Good day," she replied.

Then she would go home and start in on her homework. Some nights she slept, others she didn't. She came to school one day in October with a burning sensation that was almost unbearable when she went to the bathroom. I called the doctor. He informed me that Mary had already been treated for two severe urinary tract infections and recommended she be seen at once.

Benjamin was only able to leave his job long enough to transport her to the doctor's office. They admitted her to the hospital. I hurried over after school. I found dear Mary alone in a dim room, with an I.V. feeding antibiotics into her arm. She was crying and sobbing. I was her one and only visitor. Ironically, but not surprisingly, she was most worried about staying current with her homework and getting back to school the next day. "I can't afford to get behind, Ms. Goforth."

"You won't. I promise. But we're going to get you well first."

There is no quick remedy for kids like Mary. But love, I discovered long ago, goes a long way, and I truly loved this amazing young girl. I wrapped my arms around her, hugged her tight, and said, "It's going to be okay."

"I'm so tired of being sick, and I'm so tired of hurting. I do everything the doctors tell me to do, but I'm still sick," she whimpered.

"It's going to be alright, kiddo. I'm not going to leave you. We'll make it through this," I told her, meaning every word.

Mary had been through it all: pregnancy, arthritis, a severely cracked tooth, and three extremely painful urinary tract infections. She had watched her dad kill himself with drugs. She was witnessing her mother's spiraling decline. Most kids would have given up, but Mary refused. She was an inspiration.

After all she had been through, Mary was still in school and still working to keep her grades up. If the weather was cold, and I knew she was going to be hurting when she arrived at school, I let her curl up on my couch until the Ibuprofen took effect.

She and I never pass in the hall without sharing a hug. I tell her everyday, "We're going to get through this."

~ A Two-Way Street ~

LIKE ALL THE kids who traipse in and out of my office every day, or who sat in my classroom all those years, Mary understands my most inviolate rule: if there ever comes a time when I am doing more than the child, then it's time for me to back off. I am no different than every other teacher in classrooms across the country. I only have so many minutes in the day, and if a student isn't willing to meet me halfway, then I have to invest my time, energy, and love in a child who is willing to do his or her part. It's a two-way street. I can't have it any other way. I think of it this way; I sing in their night until they are strong enough to sing on their own. As long as they're willing to try, I'll be there.

Mary never takes our relationship for granted. She has taken so many hits in her short life, and yet she refuses to quit. She puts the well-being of her baby first and her commitment to school a close second. If I allow her to take a few extra minutes to vacate the building during a fire drill, I believe her condition warrants it. More than that, however, it reminds her that someone has her best interest in mind, and that is a great feeling.

Mary knows I am approachable. She knows I will listen to even the most intimate of her needs. All my students do. My office is a place of trust. It is also a place where the "squirrels" can come for a piece of candy and a hug. Sometimes that's all they need: someone who is easy to talk with; someone who is approachable. The highest compliment Mary ever paid me was the day she called from the doctor's office when she didn't have anyone else to be her advocate.

My goals for Mary may sound simple, but they pose a formidable challenge for someone in her situation. Best-case scenario she will graduate from high school, go on to college, and be a good mother to her baby girl.

If I have passed on to her some of the traits of a good mother and a good citizen and have given her a sense of pride in her education, then I have done my job. Will she make it? Will she find someone approachable when she moves on to the 10th grade and the trials and tribulations of high school? I can only hope.

I want her to walk away from the 9th grade knowing every problem has a solution. I want her to believe that there is always hope and that giving up is not an option.

That is exactly what I want for all my students. I have high expectations. I don't want any of them settling for second best.

~ My Worst Day ~

THERE ARE MANY times during the course of a day when a young man or woman comes by my office for nothing more than a slice of validation. All they want is for just one person to see them as more than a face in the crowd. When a student makes eye contact with me in the hall, no matter how crowded it is, he or she is asking for something: acknowledgement, recognition, a friendly smile, a ray of sunshine.

I attempt to call every student by name. If I haven't formally met a student before, I don't let them get away until I've had a look at their I.D. badge. I shake their hand, exchange some good-natured banter, and make certain they know that my door is always open to them. "Come by for a Tootsie Roll. The bowl's always full."

Validation doesn't take much more than a positive word or two.

"Make me proud, Michael."

"Nice to meet you, Amber. Holler if you need me."

"Keep up the good work, Joey. I'm counting on you."

"You better get on your grades, Ramon. I don't want to have to hurt you." I can say things like that because I've laid the groundwork. They know me. They know I'm approachable. I'm on their side, and they know that too.

Once word gets out about a safe haven or a friendly face, the name of the game becomes consistency. I can't be one way with the kids and another way with the custodial staff. I can't put on one face to meet my students and another one to meet my principal or the counselors.

Kids are watchful. They need consistency. They need predictability. Consistency and predictability breed trust. I am respectful with my fellow teachers just like I am with the on-duty police officer. The kids have to see that. They have to know that I am the same Ms. Goforth at 7:00 a.m., when they come in the building, as I am at 4:00 p.m., when I'm too exhausted to see straight.

A kid may have just left a two-room apartment where his father has been drinking all night and his brother is in the back bedroom doing meth. He spends 20 minutes on a bus hoping school will provide him with six or seven hours of sanity. When he comes into my office or takes a seat in my credit recovery lab, he should be able to expect the same energy and same genuine smile that Ms. Goforth shared with him yesterday, or last week, or the first day of school.

I once told one of my fellow teachers, "When you stop and think about it, a teacher on her worst day may be the best hope for a kid hanging on by a thread."

That's why the arts of listening and communicating are so vital, not just for an educator, but for all adults. But good communication is also a matter of consistency and predictability, and that shouldn't be too much for a child to expect.

~ Heart to Heart ~

YOU CAN NEVER see into a child's heart if you don't allow them to see into yours. If you want their heart – that insight into who they are – then you have to give them your heart. It doesn't matter if you're a teacher, a volunteer mentor, a coach, or just a friend. Connecting with a child at a deep and meaningful level requires a heartfelt commitment.

Jaime was new to our school, having enrolled after the second six-week session. Jaime's attendance was court-ordered, and I take court-ordered attendance very seriously. If a child in Jaime's situation misses school even one time without a bona fide written excuse from a doctor or a court official, it is my responsibility to investigate before filing contempt of court charges. Filing charges is not a task I relish. When it looked like it was going to be necessary to do so, I called Jaime into my office to see if this was a rectifiable situation. First, Jaime explained that his car had broken down. Then he mentioned his recent release from juvenile detention. I needed more. I said, "Do you mind telling me why you were in jail?"

Because a juvenile detainee is under no obligation to tell me about the terms of his or her imprisonment, I always phrase my inquiry in the form of a question. Interestingly, this almost always works.

"Grand theft auto," he said. "But I also stole my grandmother's social security check and broke into a couple of drug stores."

"Yep. I can see why you might have gotten sent away," I said, and he could see that I was joking. He smiled sheepishly, the way 15-year-olds do.

Then he admitted a far more serious problem. He had been a meth user. Meth is perhaps the worst of all addictions. I know this because a close relative is a user. I shared this fact with Jaime. Heart to heart. Give and take.

"I don't understand," I admitted. "I try to be there for him. I really do. But I can't fix the problem for him."

"No, you can't," Jaime agreed.

"You can't love it out of him, and you can't hope it out of him either."

"He's got to be the one to make the change." Suddenly, Jaime was leading the conversation, showing a side of himself that made him sit up a little straighter in his chair.

"How did you beat it?" I asked.

"When I went in the last time…" (referring to his last stint in jail) "...I told myself I was going to beat it. I was going to come back a different person. My mom and grandmother have always told me I'm smart. Most of my friends have already given up on school, but they're not going to talk me out of my education. Just like you can't talk your relative out of his addiction, Ms. Goforth. It's gotta be him."

This was quite a moment. Here I was, absorbing the wisdom of a 15-year-old. His insight was remarkable. I thought it was time to give him a little shove. "So what would you like to do with your life after school, Jaime?"

"I want to be a plastic surgeon."

"Wonderful. Then you need to focus on math and science," I told him.

"I'm not crazy about math," he admitted.

"You can't pursue medicine without it. You don't have to love it, you just have to do the work." A teachable moment. "But whatever you do, don't ever let anyone talk you out of your dreams, Jaime."

"I'm not. I'm going to be something, Ms. Goforth."

"Well, you're one of the most amazing young men I've ever met, Jaime. You have a lot of wisdom. Don't let it go to waste."

I told Jaime I was going to hold off on filing the contempt charge. He was surprised, pleased, and grateful. Since then, there have been no unexcused absences or tardiness. He has passed every class. I think Jaime has the strength to make it. When I say, "Make it," I don't necessarily mean as a plastic surgeon, though that may very well happen, but more as a productive member of society in some capacity.

~ You Can't Fix It ~

VERY FEW CHILDREN walk into my office expecting me to fix their problems. They don't expect the teacher standing in front of their history class to be their savior. This is a pertinent piece of information because we couldn't fix their problems even if we wanted to. We can be there with an open mind and a caring heart. We can listen. We can let them express their problems. We can empathize with their trials, and we can celebrate their victories. We can nudge them in a positive direction, and we can offer options. Taking that step in the positive direction, however, is their decision. Choosing the option is their call.

In the end, rushing to solve their problems – or attempting to do so – can do more harm than good. That is not why they come to us. Listening without judging and validating with honesty are the attributes that kick-start positive change.

The key is allowing that young man or young woman sitting across from me to believe that he or she has the wherewithal to fix his or her own problems or to deal with his or her own issues. That represents a skill that can last a lifetime.

If my only goal is to see that a child passes 9th grade, life skills might not be so important. But that is hardly my only goal. I tell a boy or girl that my goal is for them to graduate from high school and become a contributing part of my world.

~ CHAPTER FOUR ~
A Keeper of Hope Creates HOPES and DREAMS

MOST OF THE kids I work with day in and day out operate from a survival mode that is instinctual on the one hand and a product of their environment on the other. Their goals don't extend into the future. If they can make it through today, they've succeeded. The hierarchy of their needs includes a place to sleep, something to eat, and a peaceful evening uninterrupted by violence, abuse, or fear. This is not an exaggeration.

Hopes and dreams are far down their list. They have little enough to be grateful for and even less in the way of expectations. If you find yourself wondering whether you'll have a roof over your head that night, or whether you'll spend a sleepless night listening to a drunken father screaming at your mother, the future is at most a twelve-hour-window, and your one hope is that the school bus won't be late.

It's not surprising that so many kids want to throw up their hands in defeat and give up. Why keep fighting? What's the point? Why care? No one else does."

I can't relate to those questions if I don't stop and look at the world from their point of view. It's not my job to change their world, but it is my job to keep them moving forward. If I can give them a brief glimpse of a dream worth dreaming, then maybe I can instill a little piece of hope. No one wants to feel hopeless. If I can find a carrot to dangle in front of them, then maybe the future will have some promise.

The analogy I find most appropriate goes like this: I can see the light at the end of the tunnel even if my kids can't, so it is my job to get behind them and push until they see it, too. Sometimes it takes both hands and a foot.

This analogy goes hand in hand with a saying that has inspired me over the years. It is a saying I think every adult can and should relate to: "You may be the only candle in their darkness."

~ What Kids Want ~

PERHAPS IT IS easier to start this section with what children or young adults, male or female, do not want.

They do not want you to judge them by the way they look. They do not want you to see only the color of their skin or the tattoos they wear on their arms. They do not want their appearances to play into your thinking or your commitment or your attitude toward them. Kids only want you to see their souls.

Don't judge me on how well I read. Don't see me as a special ed student. Don't see the modifications I need to get through a class. Just see me as a human being.

Kids don't ask all that much from a teacher. They don't expect all that much from any adult. They are looking for someone with a positive attitude. Someone who's patient, supportive, kind, and helpful. Someone who pushes them, but who also lends a helping hand when help is needed. Someone who makes learning fun, but who recognizes their struggles. Someone who chooses encouragement over ridicule.

Here is another factor: kids can't always articulate what they want or recognize the extent of their needs. From my own personal experience, however, I think I can safely add this to our list. Kids want more than encouragement; they want someone who won't allow them to give up. They want more than mediocrity; they want someone to help them strive for greatness. Kids don't really want the adults in their lives to make decisions for them, but sometimes they have to be reminded that they have viable choices.

Children and young adults are often better at digging themselves into holes than they are at digging their way out, and that, I believe, is where concerned adults like you and me can help.

Fifteen-year-old kids often look more mature than they really are. Shaving may be a sign of physical maturity, but shaving does not guarantee intellectual and emotional maturity. Having the body of a fully-developed woman is not unusual for 15-year-old girls these days, but that physical maturity does not preclude a need for guidance in areas ranging from education and life planning to health issues and relationships. Most kids this age want guidance, even if rebellion is their middle name.

They also need a steadying hand pushing them forward: that nudge toward the light that we have been speaking about, the assurance that they are worthwhile, and the reassurance that they have something special to contribute to the world.

Ironically kids want what most of us want: patience, kindness, acceptance.

We adults should be vehicles of hope for kids. Kids shouldn't come to expect negative energy from an adult. It is incumbent upon us to make certain kids realize how special life is, how fulfilling it can be, and that they are in charge of their own outcomes. I tell my kids, "Never let anyone steal your dreams. Never let anyone tell you that you can't do something or that a goal is too big."

From a teacher's point of view, schools should be similar vehicles of hope. Coming to school shouldn't create a sense of dread. School can and should be a center of positive energy, and education that looks beyond curriculum is positive. Why? Because this view of education recognizes each student as an individual, not just a number on an attendance sheet.

If a child comes to me with the dream of being a surgeon, the very last thing he or she needs to hear is that they are aiming too high. They need to be assured, instead, that their dream is attainable. Instead of talking this child out of his or her dream, I make sure he or she recognizes in no uncertain terms the realities of becoming a surgeon. On a practical level, they should know that a surgeon-to-be can't get "C" grades in math or science. They can't miss homework assignments because they stayed out too late the night before. They can't take days off. They need to stay focused. They need to commit themselves. These are doable tasks that anyone can accomplish.

~ Planting a Seed of Hope ~

THE PHRASES "POSITIVE outcome" and "happy ending" are not generally part of my kids' vocabulary, so I have to introduce the concepts to them, one kid at a time. I have to plant the seed. A positive outcome could be something as straightforward as passing a test or seeing a star next to their name on an attendance sheet. It could be finding a part-time job after school or getting off probation. Graduating from high school might seem like a lofty goal in the eyes of some, but last year at our Central Freshman campus we had only one drop-out in a class of 850 ninth-graders.

A dream should be achievable. With the kids in my care, I can often get the wheels turning with a simple question or two. What would you like to do when you graduate from high school? How will you support yourself? What can you picture yourself doing? A cosmetologist, one girl might answer. A hair stylist, another might say. Okay, let's talk about what that means and how that dream might become an attainable goal.

The carrot I dangle in front of them has to be reachable; it also has to be realistic. We talk about the classes a would-be cosmetologist will need to take at the next level. We talk about beauty school, night classes, and internships. We gather information on the salon business. We discuss the concept of building a clientele. These are all tangible, doable steps. If the reality of what it takes to become a hair stylist is one she can grasp, and one she can picture herself pursuing, then the dream becomes a goal. Hope is the by-product.

"I'd like to be an auto mechanic," one young man tells me.

"Then you'll need an introductory course once you get to Central (the local high school). You might want to visit an auto shop, and I'll bet we can arrange that. And you'll need to research trade schools. Any idea how to do that?"

"On the Internet?"

"Now we're talking." I might also point him in the direction of the local bookstore. I might make it a class assignment. Anything to nudge him forward. Anything to plant a seed. Any carrot he might find enticing enough to chase.

~ ROTC – The Carrot That Jimmy Took ~

JIMMY WAS A tall, lanky, young man with dark-chocolate skin and a smile as rare as a four-leaf clover. He came to school hungry every morning. Thank goodness for the free meal program, because at least for lunch he was able to put something in his stomach.

Jimmy lived with an aunt. They survived on a monthly welfare check and food stamps. School was an escape and a place to be warm. He was failing every course except physical education. He rarely went a day without getting into trouble of one kind or another.

I began one of our conversations with the "what would you like to do after graduation" question, and Jimmy surprised me by saying that a career in the military topped his wish list. He said it, however, with the kind of uncertain voice that told me he couldn't imagine the Army wanting anyone like him. This was not an unusual state of mind among the many kids who passed through my office every year: when the world has beaten you far enough down, you begin to believe in your own lack of self-worth. I needed a serious jolt to convince Jimmy otherwise, so I called an officer from the high school's ROTC program and asked him to pay Jimmy a visit. He agreed to do so.

When the day came, I called Jimmy into my office, and he naturally thought the worst. The sight of a ROTC officer in uniform made an impression that Jimmy would not soon forget. They shook hands.

The officer spent a half-hour with Jimmy, talking about military life, emphasizing the virtues of discipline and self-discipline, and discussing the personal expectations a military man should require of himself. He was encouraging. He told Jimmy that he thought he had the makings of a soldier, but that he needed to bring his grades up and stay out of trouble. Planting a seed. I could have hugged the guy.

Then he issued a personal invitation to a ROTC barbeque the following weekend. "I'll pick you up myself and introduce you to the team."

Jimmy took the carrot and ran with it. He went on to Central High and was accepted into the ROTC program. School wasn't any easier for Jimmy, and life at home was still a battle of survival, but he now had something to hang on to, a glimpse of hope and a goal, both new experiences for him after 15 years.

~ Lazy as a River ~

AT 6'5", AND slender as a rail, Mark was a bona fide tall drink of water. His casual, shy demeanor was deceptive. Mark may have been the smartest young man I have ever encountered. He tested at the highest level, which unfortunately did not translate into a strong academic performance. Mark, as fate would have it, had a strong distaste for assignments in general, and homework in particular.

His philosophy toward assignments was not altogether faulty. Why, he would ask me, should I do the homework when I already grasp the concept? Logic aside, Mark was unfazed by a failing grade, and he regularly failed his classes.

He would then be assigned to my credit recovery lab, nail every in-class assignment, and then ignore every homework assignment.

Ironically Mark's enigmatic behavior seeded an idea about group testing that I presented to my principal. I suggested that we gather together thirty of my most "precious" students and allow me to administer the Texas state test that we call TAKS.

We had nothing to lose since most of these kids had never passed the state test. I was convinced, however, that it was more the psychological barriers of testing than ability. Why not put the theory to the test?

I began by telling them how excited I was. "They gave me the smartest kids in school. How much luckier could I be?"

I walked down the aisles passing out erasers and saying, "These are magic erasers. You make a mistake, the eraser erases it."

Wink, wink...

They understood that Ms. Goforth was just being her usual silly self, but most of the tension had gone out of the room by then. "Two things," I said, looking from one student to the next. "I know how wonderful each one of you is, and I know how smart you all are. So good luck. Give it your best. Make me proud!"

It went better than anyone could have expected. Not one child had to be removed from the room – a major accomplishment – and more than half the kids who had never passed a TAKS test did so this time. Mark was several points short of a perfect score. It was, as we call it, a "commended" score.

Why was this experiment successful? The kids didn't feel alienated on the one hand, instead, I believe, they felt validated and loved, which made it easier to challenge them.

If you've never tasted success, it is like a foreign concept. Once you have tasted it, the process is not so daunting. In fact, success is self-perpetuating. Suddenly, the mind-set shifts away from "can't" to "can." It may sound like a simple thing, but only if you've never walked in their shoes.

Mark spent considerable time in the alternative school called STC (Short-Term Carver). Like all students at STC, Mark was required to write a letter to an adult who had been of particular influence in his life, and I was honored when he chose me. The letter mentioned the positive aspects of our relationship, and I was touched by one particular reference. He wrote, "Thank you to Ms. Goforth. She put a smile on my face every time I saw her."

~ I See Great Things In You ~

I OFTEN WONDER what it must be like to spend your youth feeling inadequate and unimportant. When my kids are summoned to the principal's office or yanked out of class for one reason or another, they expect the worst, and they are rarely disappointed.

The questions most readily on their minds are, What have I done now? Cheated on a test? Cussed out a teacher? Started a fight?

Part of my job, as I see it, is to turn the tables on them. A "warm fuzzy," as I call it, is the last thing they expect. Sometimes I call a child into my office for no other reason than to say, "I just wanted to let you know what an amazing kid I think you are. I see something great in you. You've got the potential to go a long way. I'm really proud of you."

Yes, I see it as one of my responsibilities to encourage my kids to achieve their highest potential and to help them improve their self-image, but I have to mean the words when I say them. The expectations I have for them are not just wishful thinking. The expectations are real.

Are the kids suspicious of such praise? You bet they are. If I was a stranger with no connection to them, trying to convince them of their hidden talents, the words would go in one ear and out the other. If I was a teacher who had never bothered to say hello or shared a smile, the kids would throw up every defense mechanism in their arsenal. But this is Ms. Goforth. They may not know me, but they certainly know *about* me. I am the crazy lady who sits out front and greets them every morning. I am the chatterbox in the hall between classes. I am the one with the squirrel bowl.

They know I'm approachable. There is not one child on campus I don't care about, and I think most of them sense that. So when I tell a boy with a police record and more failing grades than passing ones that he's amazing, he can see in my eyes that it's genuine. It has to be; these kids are too hard and too cynical to fool.

I might sit across from a girl with tattoos and a pierced tongue for twenty minutes, trying to make a dent in her hard exterior. If I'm lucky enough to see one smile, it's like a gift from heaven, and I make certain she knows it.

"My goodness, you have the most beautiful smile," I might say. "Did you know that?"

She may not say "Thank you," and she may not know how to react, but I know she's smiling inside, and I know she's thinking: "She likes my smile!" And I know one other thing, too. Every time she sees me from the day on, she'll share one of her smiles.

We all respond to positive reinforcement. And for too many of these kids, a positive stroke of any kind is like an oasis in the desert. They want to believe it so badly. But a kind word is not just my way of bringing a ray of sunshine into their day. It's my way of nudging them forward. I want them to believe in themselves. I want them to know that the status quo is something from which they can break free. If I have genuinely high expectations for them, then they might come to have expectations for themselves.

Many of these kids don't expect to pass their math class or score well on their state tests. No one has every suggested to them that they might be smart, and once a lack of intelligence has been implied – no matter what the source – it's hard to break away from the label.

"You're smart. You're going to pass the TAKS test," I told one young girl the other day. She was dreading the state test. Most kids do. "You can do it. You're smart. You've got brains."

At least she would go into the state test the next day knowing that one person believed in her. Someone had used the word "smart" to describe her. She wouldn't forget it.

A 70 was considered a passing mark on the test. She scored a 72 and was ecstatic. So was I. "I told you so. Smart!"

"Smart," I have come realize, is a state-of-mind. "Smart" is a willingness to believe in yourself. "Smart" is having a dream. "Smart" is taking steps to make that dream a reality.

I believe in having high expectations for my kids. I believe we should challenge all kids to have high expectations of themselves. Encouraging them to set goals is an essential part of the process. Educational goals are important, but they should also have goals that go beyond school. Life goals.

Kids will rise to the occasion. We can help them in finding their way. Or we can hinder them.

~ Monsters ~

I THINK WE often treat kids as if their limited life experiences make them more or less able to handle the responsibilities of adulthood. In fact, kids are still kids. Special, unique, and worthwhile, but still kids, no matter what they've seen or done. I try to honor that even as I guide them toward the hopes and dreams of adulthood.

Kim was a perfect example. If ever a child fit my description of an angel to a T, Kim was it. She was petite and elfish. She had porcelain-white skin, delicate features, sky blue eyes, and blonde hair that tumbled across her shoulders in a mass of curls.

I met Kim during my first official week as an At-Risk Coordinator at Lee Middle School. She was a seventh-grader who spent most of her days in tears. She cried in the halls, cried standing in front of her locker, and cried sitting in her chair in class.

Kim, I was soon to discover, was not a victim of a troubled childhood, isolation, poverty, or drug use. Kim, in fact, came from a stable home with dedicated parents. Kim's problem was both mental and physical. She was subject to the most extreme panic and anxiety attacks I had ever witnessed. She would come to school for an hour and begin crying so intensely that the only recourse was to send her home. She had seen more than her share of doctors, but an effective treatment had yet to be found.

In the beginning, her mother and father would call me from the parking lot in the morning, announcing their arrival. I would go out to the car. I would literally peel this little girl off the back seat, take her hand, and walk her, crying and sobbing, into her classroom. There we sat. After a time, Kim would become engaged in the class activities, the crying would cease, and I would return to my office.

The fear and trepidation would return the moment class ended, the tears would begin to flow again, and we would repeat the entire process. In fact, it became so routine that her classmates no longer noticed.

"I don't know what I'm afraid of, Ms. Goforth," she must have said to me a hundred times. "I don't know why I'm so scared."

"I know, baby. That's the monster you're going to have to fight, but I swear we're going to beat it, okay?"

This was most certainly a "monster" if ever a child had to deal with one. We spent days and weeks trying to integrate Kim into a setting that eased her discomfort and fit her treatments. It was a rough, painful time. Her parents were nearly as overwrought as their daughter. They had tried numerous doctors and any number of treatments. It was a chemical imbalance that drugs often made worse. Her parents and I spoke on a regular basis, and I made certain they knew we were going to battle through this.

Kim would have spent the entire day in my office had I allowed it. But that would have been enabling an already debilitating problem. I had to get her to go to classes because learning seemed to transform her. The tears would stop. She would engage and do well.

I was battling more than just Kim's malady. I found myself at odds with some of the staff, as well. There were those who felt Kim was either faking her symptoms or exaggerating her condition. I was even forced to kick one teacher out of my office when she came in and accused Kim of manipulating the entire situation. I knew better. This angelic young lady was not in control. She had no idea what was causing the tears or what was seeding her fears.

Ironically Kim was a brilliant student. Academics were not the source of her distress. Her test scores were near perfect. She was enrolled in gifted classes that were easy for her. The fear that ruled her life had its own source, and no one could pin it down.

When Kim admitted she might possibly hurt herself, I called in her parents. Kim spent two weeks in the hospital where she was taken off one medication cold turkey – a terrible mistake – and a different medication was inappropriately crossed with another one. Kim came out in worse shape than when she went in.

After months of tears and worry, a fresh set of medical eyes determined that Kim had been given the wrong combination of drugs and had been improperly weaned from another one.

We were well into the second semester when things began to balance out. The change was slow and painful, but steady. She made it through an entire day without crying. Then a week.

When school ended and summer break began, I felt confident that Kim was on the road to recovery. The next year, I moved to Central Freshman campus, but the vice-principal at Lee kept me abreast of Kim's progress. She called me one day and said, "Debbie, you would be so proud of your little Kim. She actually performed with the choir last night in front of an auditorium full of people."

This called for an, "Oh, my goodness." I was that proud.

When school began this year, Kim's mom called and said her daughter was a little nervous about starting school at Central Freshman. I invited them in early that first day to acquaint Kim with the building. I showed her where my office was located, just in case.

Kim hasn't needed me once this year. I've gotten three or four hugs from her as I sit on my "Good Morning" perch, but she has risen above her monsters.

Kim is a success story. I can look back on those long days and hear her painful sobs and marvel at how far we've come. Now she can focus on the hopes and dreams of a budding young lady, knowing she has the power to achieve them.

~ Words Have Power ~

WHEN ADULTS SPEAK, kids hear them. It may not seem like they're listening, but they are influenced by negative words and drawn to positive ones. Teaching and mentoring children is a powerful thing. Kids can be susceptible to hurtful remarks. They often times believe the worst about themselves. It is very easy to lose their trust. But I believe strongly that we all have an inner strength that is both surprising and resilient. This inner strength helps us survive, but it also helps us thrive. After my strokes in 2000, I was told by doctors, friends, and family that it might be a struggle walking or talking. I might never set foot in a classroom again. I might never do this, and I might never do that. I refused to accept what they were saying. A little voice inside my head kept saying, "You think I won't walk or talk again? You just watch!"

After my second stroke, I lost the use of my left side; it was like my arm and leg had gone to sleep. I drew on every ounce of my inner strength. Every waking moment, I fought it. A week later, the use of my arm and hand started to return. I began walking; two or three steps at a time to regain my strength.

The cards and letters poured in from all over San Angelo. The outpouring was overwhelming, and I will never forget it. It was suggested by any number of well-meaning people that I take the semester off from school. I might want to think about withdrawing from graduate school. Stay home. Take it easy. Get well.

I said, "No. I am not missing work, and I am not putting graduate school on hold. No way, no how!"

The sympathy, as well-meaning as it may have been, would have destroyed me, had I listened. It would have robbed me of my will to fight back. Instead, I graduated with a 4.0 and hardly missed a day of work.

The strokes I suffered provided me with several valuable lessons that I impart to my students in various ways. If I think the situation warrants it, I will share the fact that I am a stroke survivor. I think it helps sometimes if they know my world isn't perfect, and that is a valuable lesson in its own right. The second lesson I share on occasion is that I am a better person in light of the strokes. It made me stronger in my heart and more focused in my goals. Lesson number three might be the most valuable of all. Perseverance: the subject of our next chapter. I didn't give up. I'm still here.

~ CHAPTER FIVE ~

A Keeper of Hope Believes in PERSEVERANCE

IT'S WISE, I think, to begin this chapter with a definition of perseverance, because it speaks directly to the obstacles and difficulties that are part of the fabric of our daily lives. Perseverance is about staying the course in spite of obstacles or difficulties. This might be a simply stated concept, but we all know that saying it is often easier than doing it.

Dreams are called dreams because fulfilling them requires us to do certain things. To make a dream an attainable goal calls for us to travel a certain path, and rarely is that a path without pitfalls. Otherwise we wouldn't call them dreams. To make a goal a reality, we almost always have to rise above certain challenges. We often have to make sacrifices. We have to be willing to stay the course whatever the obstacles. It takes tenacity. It takes a willingness to persist. All of these add up to persistence.

The challenge for me, a woman dedicated to educating kids who wake up every morning to a relatively bleak landscape, either physically, emotionally, or socially, is to recognize just how thick the walls are that they have thrown up around themselves.

When you live in a metaphoric shooting gallery – and sometimes a shooting gallery with very real bullets – the defense mechanism you're most reliant on is the one that prevents anyone from getting close to you.

I can never estimate how much time it will take to break through those walls. It might take one incisive comment about how much a young man loved his late grandmother, as was the case with Ramon. Or it might take nine months of patient interaction to draw one smile from a student consumed with grief over the death of a loved one or the betrayal of a parent.

Some kids are dying to let me in; they're just waiting for me to extend a kind word. Others may have been beaten down so many times that all they have left are their intractable ways.

I can't pick or chose. It is not realistic to set deadlines for their progress. And most importantly, I can never, ever give up. That is my golden rule: persevere until your perseverance bears fruit.

I can try and put myself in their shoes, but I can't walk in their shoes. Few of us can. The circumstances of my youth didn't prepare me to deal with the circumstances that some of my kids grew up knowing. Most of us take surviving day to day for granted, thanks to our upbringing. Our focus then was on achieving, not surviving. And for a lot of my kids, surviving is the achievement. Celebrating that achievement is a first step in breaking through their walls. Guiding them toward something of significance beyond the walls comes much later.

~ But Will You Be There When the Going Gets Tough? ~

THE AT-RISK kids I worked with during my days in the classroom, as well as those I am involved with in my current position, have one very distinct trait in common with the foster kids I cared for when I was in my 20's. None of them believe you'll be there when the going gets tough. They expect you to bail on them. It's happened before. Why not this time?

Moreover, both my at-risk kids and my foster babies would test this theory to the bitter end. They test my loyalty and my commitment at every turn. It's not a game; it's a means of survival. If they feel themselves getting too close, they push me away. They do it intentionally. On the one hand, if I'm going to walk away or send them packing, then it's over and done with, and their negative expectations are met. On the other hand, they've been stepped on and disappointed enough times that trust is just another one of the alien concepts we have been discussing.

Foster care kids and at-risk students are, in many respects, what I call "throwaways." The name comes from a rather sad realization that some adults feel it would be easier to deal with this element of society on an "out of sight, out of mind" basis. Throwaways have been hurt and rejected enough times over the years that it becomes an expectation. It is no surprise then that they expect the same from me and/or any adult who reaches out to them in good faith.

The keys are perseverance and consistency.

Kids have to know that I am not going anywhere. They're stuck with me. They can act up, misbehave, or self-destruct, but Ms. Goforth is not jumping ship. She's onboard for the duration. The importance of this is obvious, of course. Once they come to the realization that they can't push me away, an invaluable evolution occurs. Now this child is thinking, "She's going to be here regardless. She's going to stand by her words."

~ Robert ~

SOME PEOPLE LOOK at a boy like Robert, and they see a throwaway kid. Like most of the at-risk kids I've encountered, Robert did not fit the mold, and he certainly was not typical. I've heard dozens of teachers complain about students like Robert.

"I can't handle him. Get him out of my classroom."

"She's the worst kind of distraction. It's not fair to the other kids."

Fine. Send them to my classroom. I'll take them.

Robert reminded me of a sumo wrestler, both in size and strength. His skin was a rich mahogany, and his expressionless eyes were nearly as dark. He wore a buzz cut and long sideburns. His arms were decorated with black and blue tattoos.

Robert was unmistakably the toughest kid at Lee Junior High. No one messed with Robert. This rough, impenetrable exterior was Robert's one mooring. He had discovered a survival mechanism, and he put all his eggs in that one basket.

Robert was an emotional brick wall. He was an intellectual dead-end: not that he was dumb, merely intractable and unrelenting. It wasn't that Robert caused problems in class, he simply refused to do the work. "Just fail me," he would say.

I have learned that I cannot get through to every child. Some of them just won't talk. They won't make eye contact. They seem more entrenched when they leave than when they come in. I have also learned that I might actually be touching them on a different level, however, and making inroads that neither student nor teacher is aware of at the time.

Robert was one of those kids.

Robert was in my fifth period computer lab, with kids who would just as soon trash the computer as use it to research a project, finish a homework assignment, or experiment with photo art, and they were just waiting for the chance. There was still fifteen minutes left in class when Ms. Goforth faced a major crisis. I had to go to the restroom, and there was no holding it. I also knew that leaving a classroom filled with renegades was asking for trouble. I did it anyway. I was in and out of the ladies' room in record time, and not one person had moved a muscle. `I was so thrilled that I decided to show them how much I cared. Out in the hall, the kids from 5th period lunch were making a racket, so I opened the door and shouted, "Keep it down. I've got the best kids in the world in this class, and you're disturbing them."

The classroom filled with laughter. Kids were whispering under their breath and giggling. This went on for several minutes, and I thought: it was funny, but not that funny. When the bell rang, they were still giggling. Even Robert was smiling as he walked toward the door. Then he stopped.

"Ms. G.," he said. "You might want to check the back of your dress."

"Oh! My gosh!" I had been in such a hurry in the restroom that I had tucked my dress inside my panty hose. I had been flashing my class for the last ten minutes. No wonder they had been so amused. Robert, Mr. Tough Guy, was the only one who had spoken up. "Well, Robert, I guess I did it that time, didn't I? I hope everyone got a good funny out of it."

"I think they did, Ms. G.," he said and walked out.

Knowing how fast the incident would get around school, I went into the school lounge and told the principal and several colleagues that I had just flashed my computer class, and we all got a "good funny" out of it, too.

If there was an upside to the incident, it was that Robert had been compelled to come to my rescue, a minor miracle, and to initiate conversation of his own volition, something he never did with an adult.

It happened again a week later, though the circumstances were quite different. A fight broke out in the common area while I was on morning duty. It was gang-related. This was the most intense fight I had ever seen in all my years of teaching. I acted on pure instinct, plunging into the melee and shouting as if my voice might actually penetrate the rising voices of forty or fifty excited kids. When I finally broke through, I grabbed one of the combatants by the back of his shirt and threw him to the ground. I shoved his opponent against a brick wall and held on, feeling a dozen, very angry boys crowding in around me. I had expended more energy in those few seconds than I would have thought humanly possible. I was on the brink of exhaustion and just praying for reinforcements.

When I felt a hand on the back of my shoulder, I thought, "This is it. I'm in trouble now."

"Goforth." It was Robert, and his voice was as calm as a Texas evening in mid-summer.

"Yes, Robert." Mine wasn't.

"Got your back, Goforth."

"Thank you, Robert." And thank God. Here was the one kid in the whole school who could step in and hold everyone else at bay just by his presence. At the beginning of school, he would have been the last kid I would have expected to do so. Now, here he was protecting me.

Just about then, two coaches and the principal burst onto the scene, and the crowd quickly dispersed. When I turned around, Robert smiled at me for the second time in two weeks, a minor miracle.

Maybe I hadn't been able to expand Robert's interest in computer science or convince him of the importance of finishing his homework. On the other hand, maybe my perseverance had paid off in a different way. Had I chiseled away enough of the walls insulating him from the rest of the world so that Robert could see another side of himself? Had I opened him up to the vulnerabilities of his heart? Would he be willing to look at the world a little less coldly? I have to believe he will.

I have a special place in my heart for Robert. He opened me up to a different definition of the word "success." His walls never really came down, but I had made an impact I might never have seen if that fight hadn't broken out that morning or if my dress hadn't gotten caught in my panty hose.

~ The Magic Bullet ~

UNFORTUNATELY, THERE IS no such thing as a magic bullet in dealing with human beings, regardless of age, and certainly not with 15-year-old boys and girls. There are no gimmicks, and there are no pre-written worksheets. The answer lies, as I have said before, in building relationships. And relationships are built one child at a time. There is no other way. Every child is different. Every situation is unique. Few problems have the same solution.

All educators, including me, would like a book or a program that would alleviate the problems of every at-risk kid in the world. Of course, there is no such book or program. But even if there were, it would do no good if we didn't have quality teachers capable of implementing the tools spelled out in the book or the guidelines created by the program. A great teacher can take even the weakest set of tools or the cheapest program and make it a success. It's the educator, not the book or the program.

I treat every child fairly, but it is impossible to treat every child equally. Some demand more, but truly require less. Some demand nothing, and need as much as you can give.

Everyone grows at different rates. Everyone learns from their own perspectives and their own special talents. Some are auditory. Some are kinetic. Others are visual. This is not revelatory thinking by any means, but it is remarkable how easy it is to treat everyone as if they have the same world-view.

One child might not be able to write out an answer but can draw it. Then what? Teachers have to be as flexible as parents. Mentors have to approach their protégés as individuals. Friends need to embrace each other's flaws as much as they do their strengths.

~ A Question of Resources ~

TIME AND ENERGY are the most important resources I have at my disposal. I can demonstrate all the understanding and caring in the world, but there is only so much time in a day. This is not unique to the world of education; we all face the same dilemma. Sometimes I have to choose where to direct my energy. My criterion is simple. If I feel as if I am doing all the work in my interaction with a child, I have to put the brakes on long enough to say, "You're not doing your part. At this point, you need to show me that you care."

I take a step back, knowing in my heart that if I don't make this point clear to them, I am no longer an ally, I am enabling. Most kids are wise enough and insightful enough to understand the dynamics in play in such a situation. Most will acknowledge their part in the problem, apologize, and rededicate themselves. Others won't. They don't care enough to make the effort, and I can't make them care if they're dead set against it. Responsibility is not an abstract concept to a 15-year-old. They know what it means to turn in their homework on a timely basis. They understand the importance of attending their tutorials. I cannot hound them 24 hours a day. No teacher can. No mentor should have to. On the one hand, my resources don't allow it. And on the other hand, it would be a disservice to the student if I tried to.

~ Getting Too Close ~

I SPENT FIVE years in my mid-twenties as a foster parent to kids of all ages. In retrospect, the experience taught me a number of significant lessons about the at-risk students I have cared for throughout my career. Most foster care kids are starved for affection. They are starved for a safe, loving, and predictable environment simply because these are the ingredients that are most often missing from their lives.

Not surprisingly, there is a honeymoon period where these wonderful youngsters absorb every ounce of your attention. They can't get enough of your company. They thrive on the very elusive feeling of being wanted. And then, just when they feel themselves getting close, and just as their walls begin to come down, fear and apprehension set in, and they push you away. Caring for another person makes them vulnerable, and that is a scary place to be after years of rejection.

Foster kids aren't dumb. They expect to be sent away at some point. Acting-out is their way of protecting themselves. Misbehaving is an expression of distrust. Ironically foster kids have a very difficult time trusting, despite the fact that trust is something they instinctively crave. My kids at school are not so different. They've never been given a reason to trust anyone, often times not even those closest to them. It's not that all at-risk kids are rough kids, just that they are in rough situations. And it's not that all rough situations are related to poverty or drugs. Sometimes they have to do with loneliness, abandonment, or abuse. Sometimes they have to do with unrealistic expectations, or with no expectations.

Over the course of time, they see themselves developing a relationship with me. They see themselves opening up, sharing a part of themselves, and exploring uncharted personal territory. They very often counter this new-found vulnerability by reverting to their truculent ways or by intentionally breaking some rule or another.

I've learned over time that they are testing me and our relationship. They want to see the depth of my commitment and see how real our relationship truly is. Who can blame them? My response to them when they have done something wrong or stepped over the line is, "So do you really think that I think any less of you now?"

"Well, do you?"

"Sorry, kid. I'm not like that," I tell them. "You're stuck with me. I'm not backing away. We're going to keep pushing forward. I am going to stay after you whether you like it or not. You may even end up hating me. But just remember one thing, I do it because I love you."

Perseverance. There are times when resisting the urge to give up is the only reward there is. Other times, the least likely student will suddenly blossom. He or she becomes more than any of us thought possible.

Success is, however, relative for each student. I try never to lose sight of that. When in doubt, I fall back on a saying that seems most relevant when the walls a child has built are the highest and most impenetrable. "Kids need the most love when they least deserve it."

This is the child who seems the most belligerent and unruly.

This is the child who seems the most self-destructive.

This is the child who seems to court failure.

They are the ones most starved for love, and they are the ones most in need of rules, guidelines, and boundaries. And, deep down, they want the rules, guidelines, and boundaries almost as much as they want the love.

~ Peter and the Puppy ~

PETER CAME TO me in my last year at Lee Junior High. He was a tall, lanky, young man. His eyes were nearly as black as his hair. His handsome face was made even more appealing by a smile that could only be called irresistible. The girls flirted with Peter, and he flirted right back. But he was also as tough as nails. Backing down wasn't something Peter understood.

Peter was in the 8th grade when we first met, and he was failing every class. He had already been held back twice. It would not happen again. He continued to move from grade to grade now based purely on his age. It was a simple equation: 15-year-olds were not allowed in 7th grade because they were considered a distraction to kids two years younger. Sixteen-year-olds were not allowed in 8th grade for the same reason. By the time Peter got to the 9th grade, it didn't matter to him one way or another. Except for the relative stability of the school setting, he didn't care if he was there or not.

Peter's parents were both in jail on drug-related charges. He lived with his granddad. Peter did not know the meaning of supervision; he only responded to threats. Gangs, drugs, jail, and trouble were the only constants in this poor kid's life.

Here he was in 9th grade with only a string of failed classes to his credit. His path was set in stone unless someone like me could nudge him in a different direction. When Peter finally found his way to my classroom, he was hanging by a thread. He had been consigned to a 16-week drug-counseling program. He had already failed the program twice. Failure to comply a third time would mean a one-way ticket back to prison, no questions asked.

The drug program was structured around a series of mandatory classes and weekly counseling sessions. I'm sure Peter was motivated more by the fear of prison than he was by the work he and I were doing together, but he stayed drug-free for the entire four months. That was probably the longest he had been clean since he was ten.

I remember the day he raced into my classroom with the certificate documenting his successful completion of the program. He was beaming with pride. I let out a cheer and gave him a huge hug. "I knew you could do it," I said to him. I pointed to the certificate. "I'd like to share that with someone. Do you mind?"

"Sure. Who?"

"Come with me," I said with a wink.

We marched out of my classroom and down the hall to the vice-principal's office, and I could sense Peter's discomfort. You have to remember that Peter was a "frequent flyer" when it came to the vice-principal's office. He had spent a lot of quality time there, and our vice-principal was an imposing figure.

"What are we doing here?" Peter wanted to know.

"You wait here," I said, directing him to a chair in the waiting room. The vice-principal saw me coming. "What's the problem now?"

"Nothing. Nothing at all. I have something to tell you about Peter, and I need you to be supportive," I said to him directly.

This surprised him. "Okay. Bring him in."

I waved Peter inside. He was a big boy, but the vice-principal dwarfed even him. "You know Peter, of course. And I just want you to know how proud I am of him," I said, holding out the certificate. "Peter just completed a sixteen-week drug rehabilitation program, and he passed with flying colors."

"Did he?" When our school vice-principal finished reading the certificate, he stepped forward, shook Peter's hand, and looked him square in the eye. "I'm proud of you, Peter. This is fantastic."

"Thank you, Sir."

"You keep up the good work."

This was just the beginning of our work together. At this early stage, our goals had little to do with education. I was just trying to chip away at the impenetrable wall Peter had built over the years. Getting to know Peter wasn't only difficult for me. Peter hardly knew himself.

We talked about his getting a part-time job. We talked about money matters. Now that he wasn't spending every dime on drugs, we talked about ways to save money. We talked about life after school, which in Peter's case would probably happen sooner rather than later.

Some weeks after our visit with the vice-principal, Peter strolled into my classroom with a grin that made him look like a 12-year-old. Here, I thought, was a side of him I had never seen before.

"Guess what?" he said, almost gleefully. "I got a puppy."

"You? A puppy? How cool!"

"Yeah. I'm taking care of him." It was like Peter had discovered a little boy inside himself, a playful, carefree side he had never known before. "His name is Gilly. I've got these chew toys for him and a rag we play tug-of-war with."

I could picture it. The boy in the man was coming out and discovering a childhood he had never known.

"And you know where he sleeps, Ms. Goforth?" Peter cradled his arm. "Right here in my arms."

~ Pixie Dust ~

TOO OFTEN WE expect immediate results from kids who have lived at the feet of poverty and violence for the better part of their lives. Fellow teachers often send me kids who are causing problems in the classroom setting and hope they come back with a new lease on life. I can't blame my fellow teachers for that.

They are surprised and/or disappointed when I tell them I don't walk around with a purse full of magic pixie dust. It's rare when I can talk to a student one day and have them fixed the next day. The process of breaking bad habits and restoring an eroded self-confidence can be as painstaking as learning new habits and setting realistic goals.

It often comes down to perseverance. Overcoming obstacles in pursuit of dreams, goals, or even simple changes requires tenacity. It requires staying the course, and this very essential attribute applies to all of us.

~ CHAPTER SIX ~
A Keeper of Hope is a
POSITIVE ROLE MODEL

MY KIDS HAVE a term: "Sometime."

"You're a sometime friend."

"You're a sometime teacher."

"You're a sometimer."

What they are saying is that you're not predictable, you're not consistent, you're not trustworthy.

The very first time they set foot in my office I tell them, "I'm not a sometimer."

On the other hand, it's one thing to say it and quite another to demonstrate it. My kids have a built-in level of distrust, especially for anyone who fits the definition of a potential role model. The more distrustful they are, the more watchful they are. They watch everyone who has the ability to hurt them: parents, mentors, teachers, counselors. They expect to be disappointed.

In my case, they watch how I handle myself with their peers, with my own peers, with the principals and the police, with the bus drivers and the janitors. They look for consistency. They look for honesty.

If I say I'm not a "sometimer," then my actions have to back up my words. I have to be the same proactive person from 7:15 in the morning until 7:15 at night, Monday through Friday.

I have a responsibility to be a positive role model even if the kids don't recognize me as such. All teachers shoulder this responsibility, I believe, as do all adults. It's not enough to say, "Sorry, I don't want to be a role model." We are role models. The question remains as to whether we choose to be positive role models or negative ones.

Teachers have the power to lift a student up as surely as they have the ability to knock them down. Adults can push kids away just as they can draw them in and embrace their existence. A smile and a pat on the back are powerful tools. A helping hand and an encouraging word are building blocks that create ripples of positive energy.

~ Who Are You Doing This For? ~

RAY WAS TALL and rail-thin, in part from nervous energy, and in part because his main source of nutrition was the free meal program here at school. His cheeks were dimpled, his dull brown eyes were framed by thick lashes, and his narrow face was made even more narrow by the stubble of a hastily administered crew cut. He lived with his mom, but clearly she was having trouble keeping food in the cupboards.

I noticed one week that Ray's work in my credit recovery lab had come to a screeching halt. His absences were unexcused, and when he was in class, his attention was a million miles away.

I called him into my office. He sat across from me with his hands in his lap, but he couldn't bring himself to make eye contact.

"What's going on, Ray? You're one of the most amazing kids I have in class, but you've quit working. That's not the Ray I know," I said. "You know I'm not going to let you fail. Not without a fight. So tell me what's happened."

"I think I've lost my daddy." He could hardly squeeze the words out.

"Lost him how, Ray?"

"He's on probation, you know, and I haven't heard from him in a week. I think he got sent back." Back to prison, he meant. "And if he got sent back, it's for a long time this time, Miss. I just wanted to make my dad proud. But now I don't know."

"You can still make your dad proud, Ray. Your mom, too. But not if you quit working. You have to get your English grade up, and your history grade, too. You were doing so good. What happened?"

"I don't understand what's going on in that class," he replied.

"Did you ask your teacher for help?"

"I always ask for help. She said she'd already explained it three times, and she wasn't going to explain it no more. But she didn't explain it to me. She explained it to the guy next to me. But when she says stuff like that, I just give up. I just cross my arms over my chest and say I ain't doing no more for her."

This was one of those critical moments when a nudge one way or another could make all the difference. I could attack the teacher, but that would only reinforce Ray's decision to quit working. I could scold him for letting someone push him into a corner, but that would almost certainly have a similar effect.

Instead, I said, "Is that who you're doing this all for? You're doing it for your teacher? Or are you doing it for yourself? So you can make something of your life? And for your dad and mom? To make them proud?"

He was already nodding his head. "For me. And for them."

"Good," I thought. At least now the door was open. If he and I could step beyond the resistance and the rejection, we could re-focus on what was best for Ray. We could set one or two attainable goals. If I could find him a tutor who could fill the void left by his father, or a counselor willing to monitor his progress in English and history, maybe Ray would find one role model to lead him a little closer to the light at the end of the tunnel. I could see it. Now if I could just nudge Ray a little further along the path, maybe he would catch a glimpse of it, too.

I placed him with his world geography teacher, a wonderful lady who had originally come to me with concerns about Ray. Her commitment was unsurpassed. She fought for Ray the way I would have. She studied with him one-on-one. She tutored him. When all was said and done, Ray passed his semester test, which gave him enough credits to move on to high school.

~ The Story of Chief Terry Savoie ~

Chief Terry Savoie is one of my fellow teachers at Central Freshman campus in San Angelo. His is a truly moving story, and one I often refer to when I talk about positive role models, because it illustrates how influential a teacher or an adult can be in launching a child down the wrong path. I also like the Chief's story because it ends so well, thanks, in large measure, to another unlikely role model.

When Terry was in third grade, his teacher instructed all the students in her class to draw a picture of any subject they chose. They were to use a single sheet of paper and any media that struck their fancy.

That night, Terry let his imagination run wild. He drew a picture of a woman using a half-dozen different colors: green hair, blue arms, red legs, yellow feet, and bright orange hair. Terry was proud of his drawing.

The next day, his teacher hung his picture on the wall next to one drawn by a little girl named Betsy. Betsy had drawn a portrait of a smiling family standing in front of a neat and orderly house. The teacher invited Terry and Betsy to the front of the room to stand next to their pictures.

Then the teacher stood between the pair. She pointed to Betsy's portrait. "This," she told the class, "is a picture of success."

Then she pointed to Terry's multi-colored lady and said, "And this is a picture of failure."

Chief Savoie has told me numerous times how vividly that moment was burned into his memory and how strongly affected he was by this remarkably insensitive and debilitating comment.

"I was the picture of failure," he told me. "And from that moment on, I made sure I lived up to her expectations."

Terry was in and out of trouble for years. He never gave his best effort in school, and his grades proved it. "My attitude was 'Why try?'"

By the time Chief Savoie had eked his way into his junior year in high school, he had managed to fail, among other classes, algebra, not once, but three times. Fate intervened. His parents, who by now were at their wits' end, happened to strike up a conversation with a lady at the church they attended. Their conversation eventually turned to their truculent and struggling son. The woman, as it turned out, had a mathematical background, so she volunteered to tutor Terry.

"I wasn't optimistic," Chief Savoie told me. "I figured I was going to fail algebra again, and no amount of tutoring could help."

The tutor and Terry spent two weeks talking about everything under the sun except math. She was doing what all good counselors do; she was getting to know her student. Terry's interest in auto mechanics caught her attention. She went to a local mechanic and learned all she could about car engines. Then, when it came time to talk about the business of math with Terry, she tricked him into solving an algebraic formula that related to engines. This became their working model. Algebra started to make sense. The tutor planted a seed of confidence, and it blossomed. Terry passed.

He went on to graduate. The first person he called was his tutor. Being the positive role model that she was, she said, "I knew you were bound for great things."

Terry joined the Air Force. When he made Sergeant, he called her again.

He flourished. He was recognized as the United States Air Force's 1st Sergeant of the Year in 1987. He was flown to Fort Worth, Texas for a personal audience with President George Bush. When the ceremony commemorating Terry's service was over, he called her.

After all the problems Terry had faced in high school, he might have been most proud of the degrees he earned in night school in aerospace science and sociology. He celebrated every accomplishment by calling her.

When he retired after 30 years, he called her again. "I knew you could do it," she told him.

Chief Savoie became an educator. Today he is one of the most respected figures on our campus. He works with my kids as hard as I do, and he never, ever gives up on them. That's what I call a "picture of success."

That is what positive role models do. They plant seeds. They instill confidence. They show their support. They care. Chief Savoie never forgot the influence of that wonderful woman. In return, he has proved to be a role model for hundreds of kids over the years. A perfect example of "what goes around comes around."

Here is one of those stories.

~ Bucking the Odds ~

ALISA WAS THE quintessential troublemaker.

Alisa was a rough-and-tumble fighter from a family of rough-and-tumble fighters in a neighborhood ripe with every sort of negative influence a person could imagine.

Her first two years of junior high were remarkable only insofar as the number of hours she spent in detention, the amount of school she missed, and the length of the rap sheet she had with the police.

Alisa came to the Central Freshman campus with no prospects and no place to go but jail. Where the notion of joining the ROTC program came from, I never really knew. I did know that Alisa had a built-in resentment of authority, and I knew the head of our ROTC program, none other than Chief Terry Savoie, was an authority figure if ever there was one.

But Chief Savoie didn't judge people on their past behavior, only on their current aspirations and their willingness to embrace the program. The results in Alisa's case were amazing.

The ROTC uniform had a magical affect on Alisa. The very first time she put it on, she seemed to be infused with a new level of respect, both for herself, and the world around her. She carried herself differently. She walked with a sure step and an air of confidence. She began passing her classes. Her perpetual visits to the office and detention were suddenly things of the past. I could see her future opening up in front of her.

Wednesdays were ROTC days: full uniforms, drills, inspections. These were full-blown inspections at the hands of a 30-year Air Force veteran: put your hair up, shine those shoes, stand tall, and look me in the eye. And most of all, be proud of yourself and your uniform. Alisa was a natural. She was fast becoming a model of ROTC leadership.

At the end of our third six-week session, I didn't see Alisa at ROTC day. She missed one inspection and then another. I found out that she had gotten a schedule change. I couldn't understand it. She had been doing so well. She had transformed herself. I went to Chief Savoie and asked why Alisa had been kicked out of the program. What other explanation could there be?

"I didn't kick Alisa out, Debbie," Terry assured me. "She quit."

"Quit? What happened?"

Terry told me the story. Alisa's mother had stormed into his classroom one day demanding to know why Terry was teaching her daughter that she was better than her mother. "How dare you! All of a sudden she's starting to make her bed up and clean up her room. Saying 'Yes, ma'am' and 'No, ma'am' to me. How dare you teach her that she's better than me!"

I was appalled. "What did you say?"

"I said, 'All I'm trying to do is teach your daughter to respect herself. All I'm trying to do is teach her to be proud of who she is.' And she said, 'Well, I won't have it.' She made Alisa drop out of ROTC."

Terry and I had both seen it before: parents who can't stand to see their children with hopes and dreams of their own, parents who can't bring themselves to support positive behavior, parents who don't have the strength or courage to wish better lives for their kids. I will never understand it. Sad hardly describes it. Tragic.

I tried to keep Alisa from reverting back to her truculent ways, but it was not to be. There is only so much that I, or any other adult, can do in the wake of outside influences like the ones Alisa encounters every day. Soon enough, she was skipping school again, causing trouble when she was here, and clashing with the law when she wasn't here.

As positive a role model as Chief Savoie had proved to be in Alisa's life, his efforts were undermined by the insecurities of her mother. Is it possible that the lessons Alisa learned from her short involvement with ROTC, and the mentoring she received from Chief Savoie, will surface again in the future? I believe they will, because I believe the efforts and influence of positive role models becomes part of our being. We might be forced to suppress them, the way Alisa was, but the next time she has a chance to use those lessons, they'll be there. I couldn't go to work tomorrow if I didn't believe that.

~ Teddy ~

I HAVE KNOWN Teddy since he was in the 7th grade, when I was in my first year as the At-Coordinator at Lee Junior High in San Angelo, Texas. I called him "Little Teddy." The nickname wasn't entirely accurate. Teddy was short, but he was also pudgy and pugnacious. Teddy looked out at the world through sad, puppy-dog eyes. His long, stringy hair hung well below his ears. When he smiled, his cheeks swelled like melons.

Teddy had not yet been diagnosed as a special needs child, but I could see he had problems that weren't part of his official file. He fell asleep the minute class started. He didn't just doze off. He fell into the deepest, darkest sleep you could ever imagine. It was coma-like, to the point where rousing him was nearly impossible. I knew this wasn't just a 13-year-old staying up too late at night. This was a physical problem. I wanted to call in his guardian, but it was hard to determine who this was. According to his file, he didn't live with his mother. He had spent some time living with his grandmother and uncle, but now seemed to be in the care of an aunt. The only number I had was for the mother, however, and when I finally got hold of her, I urged her to take Teddy to the doctor. Gratefully, she did. I say gratefully because often times the parents of my kids – if their parents are even active in their lives – either don't care or don't have the means. Teddy's mom happened to be insured under Medicaid.

Teddy was diagnosed as diabetic. His blood sugar count was a staggering 550. He was suffering from oxygen deprivation, and the result was the dangerously deep sleeps into which he fell. He was sent to the hospital and ended up spending an entire week there.

Teddy has been on insulin ever since. He doesn't fall asleep in class any more, at least not every day. He is in charge of reading his own blood sugar and watching his diet, but when you come from the kind of poverty that Teddy has always known, often times the only foods his family can afford are beans and potatoes, straight carbohydrates that turn to sugar the minute the body starts to digest them.

I couldn't do anything about Teddy's diet away from school, but I could make certain he was on the free meal program at school. I also helped him monitor his blood sugar. We discussed the meaning of sanitation and how important proper hygiene was around needles. These were all lessons he should have gotten at home, but didn't.

Like so many kids, Teddy was starved for even a single person to reach out to him: someone who would listen, someone who could provide a calming influence in his sea of turmoil. Most of my at-risk kids are hungry for this very thing.

It is a very fine line that any adult walks between being a productive role model wanting to validate a child's existence and over-reacting to their needs and wants. We have talked about the power of empathy, and I have often found that empathy requires me to share their tears. But empathy may also require showing no emotion. It often means playing the strong-willed soldier whose singular task it is to help a child deal with his or her problems. Find a solution, encourage them to act, and send them back out into the hard, cruel world. I can't tell you how often I have closed my office door and crumbled. The pain I feel for some of these kids and their struggles is so real that I have to release it. Either release it or let it tear me up inside.

But I know one thing for certain, and I will repeat it often in this book. Sympathy is not beneficial. The minute I allow my feelings to slip from empathy into sympathy, I am of no use to them. Empathy demonstrates my understanding. Empathy allows us to work together.

In Teddy's case, it would be easy to say that he has almost no chance, given the string of hits life has delivered to him, but he just needs one person to believe in him. How many 15-year-olds have been in so much trouble that they're been assigned a parole officer? How many kids his age have been taken from their drug-addicted mother because she was deemed incapable of caring for him and his siblings? How many kids have suffered a breakdown and been confined to a mental institution? How many kids are shuffled from one relative to the next in hopes of finding at least one person who cares about their well-being? Teddy's aunt may have wished the best for him, but she could hardly take care of herself, much less three kids who didn't belong to her.

It was my job to call Child Protection Services and report what I knew. Teddy was out of insulin, and he could die because of it. He and his siblings were often being left at home alone, and not just for an hour or two, but for days at a time. They lived in a house without heat or electricity. His diet was out of control; he either had no food or the wrong kind of food. So I placed the call.

I would give anything if Social Services could find Teddy a foster home with a father and mother who could offer him a sense of place and stability and, maybe for the first time, a sense of self-worth. Teddy deserves that chance.

~ Hope Is Making the Hard Calls ~

HOPE IS THE best of all gifts, and it is one thing Teddy has rarely known. Hope is the one thing I try and bring into the lives of my kids. Calling Child Protection Services may sound like a last resort, but it was a call I had to make. I can advocate for Teddy at school, but CPS and Social Services offer him his only chance of rising above an otherwise hopeless situation outside these safe and warm walls.

There are often hard calls that have to be made about the kids who pass through my office every day, but it is the small gestures that sometimes have the most lasting effect. A simple smile goes a long way. A few words that acknowledge to kids their importance are invaluable.

There are occasions when I have to do things that leave me looking like the bad guy in a kid's eyes. There are times when a call to an agency like CPS is in their best interest even if it doesn't seem like it on the surface. It pains me to do it, and I sometimes find myself the recipient of a kid's hatred or anger.

Every time, I respond the same way. I tell them, "If there is a chance of you hurting yourself or someone else, or if there is a chance of you not being in my world, then I'd rather get you the help you need and take you hating me. I'll pay the price. I have to have you in my world." Period. End of story.

~ Tina ~

TINA HAD A list of distinguishing characteristics, some more positive than others, but all of them endearing to me.

Tina was a cute, dimpled girl. She was blessed with the curliest chestnut hair I had ever seen, and it rose and fell with every step she took. The hair seemed to fit her temper, which was legendary among the staff at Lee Junior High. To her credit, Tina recognized her temper to be a serious problem and always took responsibility for it once she calmed down. I spent many sessions talking her down and many other sessions exploring the source of her volatility. I used every technique in the book, from play-acting to journaling. What it came down to in the end with Tina was presenting myself as someone she could trust, someone she could speak freely with, and someone who refused to judge her based upon her behavior.

Tina, I discovered, came from a violent family. She was able to admit that after a time, but she didn't blame her situation on that dynamic.

Her father was in prison, and her mother had spent more than her fair share of time behind bars. Not outstanding role models. Tina, however, refused to hold a grudge or blame them for her plight.

I admired Tina for that, but, in reality, she had grown up in a situation where raised voices and verbal aggression were the rule of thumb. She was a product of that environment, and it probably didn't include a great number of positive role models.

Our work together focused on Tina's personal insecurity and the scarcity of trust she had experienced over the years. Every time Tina tried to express herself or make her needs known at home, she would be trumped by louder voices.

She longed to be viewed as an equal. I told her she deserved nothing less. She longed to be heard. I showed her that speaking calmly and softly was far more effective than shouting.

"Shouting puts people on the defensive, Tina. Shouting alienates people," I said. "And it also demonstrates a lack of confidence. And I know you have more confidence than that."

I didn't come right out and tell her that a quiet voice exudes confidence, or that a calm voice engages people and draws them in. I tried to let my actions speak for themselves. Speaking softly is a technique I employ every day. The more tense the situation, the more calmly I speak. I wanted Tina to experience this without making it sound like a directive.

Tina had an advantage. She wanted to succeed. She wanted to rise above her environment, and she was smart enough to grasp the concepts we were discussing. We set goals for her academic year, and she exceeded each and every one of them. Toward the end of the third six-week term, she came into my office and presented me with a home-made certificate proclaiming me "Counselor of the Year at Central Freshman."

It didn't matter to either of us that I was not a counselor. It was an honor. It signaled the progress Tina had made.

I didn't invite Tina into my office thinking, "This is a child who needs a positive role model," even if it were true. I invited her into my office hoping to give her a view of the world that went beyond her environment at home and on the streets. But when you think about it, the two go hand in hand.

By the time Tina had enrolled at Central High the following fall, she had traded her temper for a more confident persona that made me think she had turned the corner. As for me, I hung my "Counselor of the Year" certificate on the wall of my office, and it remains there to this day.

~ CHAPTER SEVEN ~

A Keeper of Hope Values ACKNOWLEDGEMENT

WHEN WE ACKNOWLEDGE another person – man, woman, or child, without regard for circumstances good or bad – we are essentially saying that man, woman, or child has value.

When I am speaking to an audience of teachers, educators, or parent groups, I use a simple game of audience participation to demonstrate this concept.

Step one: enticing a volunteer from the audience.

Step two: taking a twenty-dollar bill from my purse.

I hold up the bill for all to see and then say to my volunteer, "Would you like this twenty-dollar bill? No questions asked"

Answer: "Sure. Why not? Absolutely."

"I thought you'd say that." Then I wad the bill up and ask the same question. "Do you still what it?"

"I still want it."

Then I throw it in the trashcan. "And now?"

"I still want it."

Then I take it out of the trashcan and spit on it. "And now?"

My volunteer may shudder a bit at this, but he or she always says,

"I still want it."

Then I throw the bill on the floor, stomp on it with my shoe, and twist the heel into it. "Do you still want this twenty-dollar bill?" I ask.

"I still want that twenty-dollar bill," the volunteer assures me.

So I ask, "Why"

"It's still good."

After I unravel the bill and pass it on to my volunteer, I look out at my audience and very quietly say, "My kids are like that twenty-dollar bill. They have been wadded up. They have been stepped on. They have been spit on, stomped on, and thrown away. But you know what? They still have value. They are still children on the inside. We can't take that away from them just because life has beaten them down at every turn."

More than just recognizing this, it is absolutely vital to acknowledge their worth. It is necessary to recognize that they are still adults in training. How often are we tempted to say, "Why in the heck don't they grow up?"

The truth is, that is exactly what they are doing. They are in the process of growing up. This is their time to make mistakes. Isn't that worth acknowledging? This is the time for you and me as teachers and adults to make the most of every "teachable moment." This is the time when these kids are learning right from wrong, and when they are growing, learning, changing, and exploring.

It is our job as adults to acknowledge every child's value as a human being. It is our job to acknowledge their accomplishments even as we assist with their problems. It is our job to acknowledge their dreams even as we are trying to instill them with hope.

Through it all, they still have value.

~ A Diamond in the Rough ~

A BOY CAME into my office the day after receiving his grades from the last six-week session. I could see by his expression and posture that he was not happy.

I said, "Frankie. One of my all-time favorite students. What's going on?"

"I messed up," he said glumly.

"Okay. How'd you mess up?"

"I failed two classes."

As odd as it may sound, I saw an opportunity presenting itself, a chance to acknowledge Frankie's progress and validate him as a maturing adult. I said, "Outstanding. I'm proud of you. Oh, my gosh."

He was perplexed. "Ms. Goforth. I failed two classes."

"And how many classes did you fail last session?"

"Six."

"Okay. So last session you failed six classes," I said. "This six-weeks you failed two. That means you repaired four classes. You grew. You made progress. I'm proud of you."

"Yeah," he admitted. "I guess I did make some progress."

"And here's another thing. At the beginning of the year would you have felt comfortable coming in here and talking to me about your grades?"

"No way. I didn't give a flip about my grades then," he said.

"So it sounds like we have a couple of things to celebrate," I told him.

It is important to remember that Frankie's success is relative to his circumstances, but it is still a success. Success means something different for every one of us, and it's neither fair nor wise to assume that anyone else is marching to the beat of your particular drum. Frankie was growing, working his way through the fragile maze of his precarious world, and it was my responsibility to get the most out of that growth.

As I said earlier, I don't walk around with a pocket full of magic pixie dust. No teacher does. No mentor or friend does. I can't change a 15-year-old's suspect behavior, and the negative impact of poverty, gangs, and drugs, overnight. Kids are individuals. It's neither fair nor constructive to compare one child and his circumstances with those of another child.

~ LeAnn ~

SOME TEACHERS HAVE a magic touch. They can see the slightest change in a student's demeanor, a shift in his or her attitude, and even the weight of the smallest distraction.

LeAnn's history teacher was one of those. Much like Ray's teacher, she came to me and said, "There's a problem. I know it. She could use a friendly voice and some personal attention if you're available."

That very day, I invited LeAnn into my office. I could see even without asking that she was teetering on the edge of something more traumatic than a missed homework assignment, but sometimes it's best to prime the pump with a minor matter and hope the student opens up. With this in mind, I said, "I hear you're having a hard time getting your homework finished, young lady. Is there something going on? Something I can help you with? That's why I'm here, in case you didn't know."

"It's not anything like that," she said. "It's my mom."

The way LeAnn said, "It's my mom," I knew this wasn't a mother/daughter conflict. There was a sadness in her voice that told me this was much more serious. I could also tell that she was almost desperate to share whatever her burden was.

"What is it, LeAnn? You can tell me."

"She's in the hospital. She's got cancer. She's dying."

Oh, my gosh! Of all things, not that. But saying the words helped her. I could see that. "Oh, sweetheart, I'm so sorry," I said. I wanted to keep her talking.

"The doctors say only six weeks."

The tears came, and we both cried. Then we talked. We talked about how difficult it was for her twin brothers and her father. This allowed LeAnn to show her strength and pride. Then we talked about taking it one day at a time. This allowed her to move forward without being totally overwhelmed. Teachable moments.

LeAnn was spending every evening at the hospital. Even her mom was encouraging her to say focused at school. But homework was not a priority. Facing life without her mother was. So I traded my compassion hat for my guidance hat and asked LeAnn if it was all right if I spoke to her teachers in confidence about her situation and asked for their understanding regarding her assignments. LeAnn was grateful. Her teachers appreciated the insight. It helped.

LeAnn's mother died 12 days later. I called to express my condolences, but also to let LeAnn know that I was there if she needed me. LeAnn wouldn't talk to me. I understood. She had put up her walls. She was in survival mode, and surviving meant being as strong and as tough as she could be. LeAnn hadn't learned yet that letting down your guard was one of the strongest things a person could do.

She avoided me in the halls. She wouldn't make eye contact. It was fine. I would bide my time. When she was ready, I would be there.

Three weeks later, she knocked on my office door. She walked in, took one look at me, and started sobbing. I folded my arms around her and let her cry. When the tears slowed, she apologized for crying. I said, "You're grieving. You have to feel the loss. My mother died seven years ago, and I still cry when it hurts. But isn't it wonderful that we loved someone so much?"

"Yeah. It is wonderful."

LeAnn and I talked more about life and death, grieving and loss, and the tiny steps that allow us to move forward.

I worked with LeAnn and her teachers over the next months, and she passed every class that year. Looking back, I realized that had it not been for one teacher taking a special interest in LeAnn and reacting to the change in her demeanor, she may well have fallen through the cracks. Her situation may never have come to light. We might never have been able to offer the support we did.

I applaud teachers who take the time to acknowledge their students as individuals with individual needs. Teachers who are connected, caring, compassionate. Teachers who are making a difference.

~ Bells and Whistles ~

WE TEACHERS ARE notorious for assigning elaborate projects that call for all sorts of props and materials, as if every student in class can go to the local hobby shop for paints, paper, and glitter. We often end up passing out grades based upon bells and whistles, fluff and fizzle, instead of upon content and creativity.

Grading based upon the amount of money a kid's parents are willing to spend, even if it's not intentional, is tricky business at best. A nickel in the hands of one student might seem trivial; in the hands of another student, it might seem like a small fortune.

Thomas Jefferson once said, "Nothing is more unequal than equal treatment of unequal people." I think what he was saying, as it applies to the Central Freshman campus, was that there are a lot of factors that influence the treatment of 850 ninth-graders from every possible walk of life. The challenge for teachers is to view every child in the classroom as a unique individual, and that is not easy to do.

In a perfect world, it would be incumbent upon teachers at every level to search out each student's strength, his or her area of interest, and make every effort to identify each student's unique learning style.

In an imperfect world, maybe acknowledging a student's inherent value is a starting point we can all accept. Bringing their gifts to light gives substance to their value and hope for the future.

Still, it begins with acknowledgement. That is always doable.

~ Second Chances ~

THE A+ LABS, as we call them, are where we at the Central Freshman campus conduct our credit recovery program. Credit recovery allows a student six weeks to bring a failed grade up to a passing one. And while this has a purely academic ring to it, the program is really about second chances. How does this fit into our discussion about acknowledgement? When we acknowledge that a child deserves a second chance, we give them hope. Giving them hope is another way of validating their worth. It's a way of saying, "You deserve to succeed!"

I don't believe that any child arrives on campus the first day of school expecting to fail every class. With a few exceptions, I think most kids come to school hoping to do well, "well" being a relative term that is different for every student. Very few students aspire to a cycle of failure. I have to believe that.

Yet sometimes things happen over the course of a year: issues at home, issues with basic survival, issues with self-esteem. When these issues put a child's status at school in jeopardy, when they fail a six-week session in history or English or math – whatever the class – they are given a second chance to "repair" that grade in one of my A+ labs. The labs are all computer-based, and the program has a positive twist to it. If a student answers a question correctly or completes a problem successfully, a computerized thumbs-up image appears on the screen and a voice exalts: "Good job," or "Way to go," or "Outstanding." If the student gives an incorrect answer, the computer has several responses: "Sorry," or "Try again."

This is not only positive, it is pragmatic. It allows each student to work at his or her own pace. It is a win-win situation.

When a student successfully "repairs" a failed grade, I go old-school on them and hang a star from the ceiling. I make an announcement, and the entire class cheers. You might think a rough-and-tumble ninth-grader would find a little star cut out of construction paper silly, but you'd be wrong. Their excitement is as real and palpable as a kid half their age. I cannot tell you how many times a boy or girl has stopped me in the hall and asked me if I've put up his or her star yet.

What does that tell you?

That silly star is an acknowledgement of a successful accomplishment, no matter how small. It's validation. It says, "I did something good." It's my way of bragging on their behalf. It's my way of promoting a sense of belonging.

There is not a person alive who doesn't want to belong, and I think it is the responsibility of every adult to make sure that a child has a place in which a sense of belonging exists. It could be a club, a sporting activity, or a safe and inspiring classroom. It could be a part-time job, a church group, or an after-school recreation center. The key is to find a place where failure is not an option.

The alternative is to let them find a sense of belonging as a member of a gang or to let them look for validation and acknowledgement on the streets. The alternative is loneliness or isolation. And those aren't acceptable alternatives at all.

~ An Apple a Day ~

MOST OF THE kids I see in my at-risk position are nearly incapable of acknowledging their own successes. That's where I come in. Positive behavior is something I acknowledge whenever the opportunity arises, and the occasion need not be earth-shattering. Passing even the simplest lesson is worthy of celebration. When a child sits across from me, I dig for even the smallest accomplishment, and then acknowledge it in typical Goforth style: part silliness, part grandiosity, all sincerity. I call it "getting an apple." The apple, either figuratively or literally, is a sign of achievement.

In the A+ labs, the apple is the symbol that appears on the computer screen signaling a successful completion.

When I shout, "Yahoo! We've got an apple here," it might cause a moment of embarrassment, but the embarrassment is really pride, and it is a wonderful gift. These kids know my expectations are high for them, and they will often come all the way across campus to tell me, "I got an *apple* in lab today."

An "apple" in this context may be an acknowledgement of a completed assignment, but it is also a means of validation. It is a sign of hope.

And where there is hope, there are dreams. Having dreams for the future is something you and I take as a given. Dreams are part of our lives; they give us something to work toward. Not so for a child who is just trying to get through the day. The gift of a dream is priceless. Often it starts with something as simple as an apple.

~ Trey ~

TREY WAS A veteran of prison life by the age of 15. He had served two terms by the time he and I crossed paths. As an At-Risk Coordinator, I make an effort to acquaint myself with every student with a police record, and Trey's wrap sheet read like a hardened criminal's.

He had a tattoo of a tear on his face; it hung like a purple drop from the corner of his eye. Yet as hard as Trey was, and as deep as he was into the world of crime and gang activity, I still looked at him as one of my kids.

Most people would look at someone with Trey's learning deficiencies – he was enrolled in classes where the curriculum focused on the most basic of skills, like dental hygiene and reading street signs – and figure there was no hope. Yet in my eyes, Trey was like any other young man or woman. He and his generation are my future. These are the kids who will be taking care of my generation when we're older. Trey deserves as much kindness as the straight-A student or the star quarterback. I want the Treys of the world to be productive, involved citizens.

Over time, Trey and I developed a relationship. His dark, round face rarely smiled, but when he did, his cheeks dimpled, and his eyes lit up. And when the subjects of the Army and ROTC came up, Trey smiled.

"But he won't take me," Trey said, in reference to the school's ROTC director, Chief Terry Savoie.

"Have you talked with Chief Savoie, Trey?" I asked.

He shook his head. "I don't have to. They don't take anyone with tattoos on the neck or face."

"If you're serious about the program," I said, "I'll talk to him. Maybe there's something we can do."

Chief Savoie not only invited Trey to sit in on a ROTC meeting, he had a simple solution for his tear tattoo. He covered it with a Band-Aid.

This only solved half of the problem. Trey was 15, and he couldn't read.

I wanted Chief Savoie to appreciate the commitment he was going to have to make to Trey, although he was the kind of educator who gave his all to every student, regardless of the circumstances. He was not only willing to work with Trey, he was eager to do so.

We both understood that Trey would probably never make it in the Army, given his learning disabilities, but the skills he would learn in ROTC would almost certainly last him a lifetime. That was sufficient motivation for Chief Savoie.

I have to admit that I became slightly teary-eyed the day Trey showed up in his new uniform. The transformation in his posture and the gleam in his eye were nothing short of miraculous. I believe that in that one moment that Trey caught a glimpse of the man he could be; I believe he saw, at least briefly, beyond a life of crime and gangs and cell bars.

Six weeks into the term, I was informed that Trey had been in a serious fight. Apparently he had not initiated the altercation, but he had clearly ended it: that is to say that his opponent was in far worse shape than Trey was.

I pulled Trey out of his special ed class. He wouldn't look at me. He found a spot on the floor and fixed his eyes to it.

"I heard you were in a fight, Trey. Is that true?"

"Yeah." He shuffled from one foot to the other.

"Well, here's the thing, Trey. You don't know me very well yet, but you need to understand that I don't give up on people. Okay?" He didn't answer. "Listen, this fight you were in is like anything else. It's a learning lesson in life. Do you think I think less of you because you were involved in a fight?"

"Yeah, that's exactly what I think. We're done being friends because I messed up. That's the way it works."

"Wrong. That's not the way it works with me." I took his face gently in my hands and drew his eyes to mine. "You're stuck with me, kid. I'm not going to give up on you. Hear me?"

Trey may have been a juvenile delinquent and a car thief. His dad and his brother may have been locked up somewhere, and his mother may have been working the streets, but he was still only 15 and a kid. Kids hurt. Kids are desperate for someone to believe in them. He bit down on his lip, but he couldn't fight off the tears. His eyes filled and spilled over. His shoulders shook. I held him a moment and let him cry. I could tell how cathartic it was; I could tell that he had been holding back those tears for a very long time.

As badly as Chief Savoie and I wanted to change the direction of Trey's life, and as much as he may have wanted a normal life, it was not to be. The odds were stacked against him, and there was a limit to what we could do. Come summer, he was behind bars again.

~ Adults in Training ~

I cannot better summarize this chapter on acknowledgement than to remind you that some of these kids might have the physical maturity of adults, but they are not adults, not yet. They are adults in training. Acknowledging that they are adults in training is a vital first step in assisting them toward adulthood and giving them the tools of successful adults. It makes our job easier, and it makes the road they have to travel a little less treacherous and a little less daunting.

~ CHAPTER EIGHT ~
A Keeper of Hope is a GUIDING LIGHT

GUIDANCE IS THE fine art of helping a child find his or her own path.

Guidance is more the process of assisting a student in their search than it is forcing them to see what you want them to see. When a boy or girl is fifteen, there is a great and dynamic world that seems as unfamiliar as it is enticing, as exciting as it is fearful. On the rosy side of this spectrum are kids who look at the unknown with enthusiasm and optimism. On the other side are those who lack the confidence to explore even the fringes of the unknown. How do we give guidance to the former while inspiring the latter? Some have the benefit of loving parents and willing teachers to point them in the right direction and to alert them to the obstacles. Others may have grown up with no parents at all or with parents who help create the obstacles. How do we give a sense of perspective to the former while creating positive experiences for the latter?

Guidance is about recognizing opportunity and glimpsing the future. But sometimes guidance is less glamorous than that and is more a matter of practicality. Sometimes guidance is making certain a student is aware of the consequences of failure. Other times it is about making them aware of the consequences of success. And just as often, in the case of many of the kids I counsel every day, it is about making sure homework assigned on Monday is turned in on Tuesday.

If a child's highest priority is filling his stomach at least once during the course of a day, then I have to make certain he has swallowed his pride and signed up for the free meal program. If a kid is facing the possibility of court-ordered attendance, then I have to make sure he or she is fully aware of the consequences of skipping school or unexcused tardiness. If a student is on the verge of being held back a grade, I have to begin doing things like checking on his or her grades throughout the term, not just at the end of the six-week session. I have to stay on them about pending assignments and class attendance. I have to talk with them about taking responsibility for their actions. I have to instill in them a sense of consequences. It may sound like babysitting, but I don't see it that way. It's my way of guiding them one assignment at a time, one class at a time, and one day at a time.

Most of us have helped a toddler take his or her first steps. It's an extraordinary process. We help them pull themselves up using the leg of a chair or the edge of a couch. We offer them our finger for balance and support. We cheer each victory, no matter how small the step. But eventually we have to let them venture forth without the aid of our finger, even if it means taking a tumble or two. We help them up and send them on their way. It's not long before they are no longer seeking the support or the balance. It's not long before walking is as natural as crawling once was. Soon they're running.

Guidance is like that. It isn't just a matter of steering them down a path that stretches into the future, it's a matter of helping them negotiate the forks in the road. I can't be their parent, but I can be a campus parent, and offering guidance is part of the job.

~ Todd's Story: I Can't Fix It ~

TODD IS A football player. He looks like a football player. He carries himself like a linebacker. Todd was hard not to like. He never bullied anyone. He never talked down to anyone. He may have been an average student, but he worked hard. He showed up. He was consistent with his assignments.

So when he fell behind midway through the second semester, I wasn't the only one who started to worry. His math teacher came to me and said, "Something's going on. He's not smiling. It looks to me like he's got the weight of the world on his shoulders."

She was right. And when I saw the sadness in Todd's eyes as he walked down the hall that March day, I invited him into my office. I closed the door and offered him a Tootsie Roll from my squirrel jar. I sat across from him, but he couldn't meet my eye.

I said, "Where's that smile been the last couple of days, young man? I've missed it." When he didn't answer, I dug a little deeper. "You want to talk about it, Todd? What's going on?"

Todd could cry in my office because he knew no one was around, and he knew me well enough to know that my office was a place of complete confidentiality. He told me his story.

His family had driven to San Antonio recently in preparation for his father's scheduled deployment to Iraq. Saying goodbye was hard enough. But the trip to San Antonio was also a chance to take his sister Cindy to the military hospital. She had been sick for some time. The family had been home-schooling her. The diagnosis wasn't good. The doctors told the family that Cindy was going to be blind, probably within the next six months.

"And I can't fix it," he kept saying. "My dad's gone, and I'm the man of the house now. And I can't fix it."

I told this amazing young man two things I thought he needed to know right then and there. I told him to remember that his dad was still his dad, and still the head of their household, and that he didn't expect his 15-year-old son to take on all his responsibilities. "You have to keep being a kid, too. You have to keep being 15, because that's something your dad would want you to do."

I also told him that while he was being strong at home, strong for his mother and his sister, that he might need someone to be strong for him every once and a while, and I was here for him.

I knew that Todd might not take me up on my offer, but it couldn't hurt knowing someone was available to him.

Guidance has so many dimensions, but allowing a child to know he or she has more than one choice is one of the most invaluable of all.

~ Failure is Unacceptable ~

IN TWENTY YEARS, few students will be able to remember who taught them the key components of a right-angle or a trapezoid. Few will remember which teacher explained the difference between a verb and a noun.

What they will remember is who their favorite teacher was back in grade school, or who their least favorite was in junior high. What they will remember is how that particular teacher, good or bad, earned that distinction. And the how is the same in both cases. It's a question of how did that teacher make you feel in the classroom? The least favorite one may have made you feel fearful, unappreciated, rebellious, or even worthless. The favorite teacher may have made you feel enthusiastic, comfortable, successful, or simply capable.

This tells me that educators are responsible for much more than just the curriculum, as we have discussed earlier. The curriculum is the easy part. We all have lesson plans and pacing guides. Building a relationship is the difficult part. Once we've done that with each and every child in the classroom, the rest falls into place.

As an educator, I realized that once I had developed a relationship with my students, male or female, I felt comfortable telling them that failure was unacceptable. I felt confident saying, "You're going to stay with me until you get it. You're not walking out of my class without having learned."

Guidance goes beyond the lesson plans and the results of standardized tests.

Guidance is a matter of life, and life lessons.

~ How Will You Create Tomorrow? ~

I ALWAYS INCLUDE in my discussions surrounding guidance a wonderful paper written by a dear friend of mine, Nathaniel Slawson. It goes like this:

> The future we are all destined to live will be fashioned by the hands of children…

> Set before our eyes, this world remains forever born of tomorrow, delicately bonded to each hope, dream and wish we gently raise aloft to place upon the coming dawn. It is in that day, when your strength has begun to fade and you must rest the work of your life over the arms of youth, in that painfully sweet day of surrender you will see life bow to the effort your hands have given…

Returned in kind by those you have helped to grow.

Teaching is not simply a profession; it will suffer no amount of time nor suffer any exhausted effort to bring degradation against the truth of its sanctity. It is the work of a teacher that creates and binds the prospect of things to come. This simple honesty is founded not in what you educate but in how you educate…

Tomorrow's prominence is decided today, decided in the hearts and minds of the children that fill your classroom, that laugh in your hallways, that search your words for their own validity and cry out for guidance that only you can give. The very same hands that collect books from atop your desk, the very same voices that call out hopeful answers, and the very same eyes that seek knowledge…will become the ones who lead us.

Our children will lead not by any manner of right, nor any manner of fate…they will lead by the world they have been shown…they will lead by how you have taught them. They will lead by the bond you have given them.

Tomorrow's wars and times of peace are decided today, decided by the care you take, the time you offer, the shelter you become and the love you give.

Each child you grant passage from the darkness of uncertainty into the light of knowledge will make a difference, their impact will be felt without regard to our imaginations, without regard to what we believe they may become…their impact on will be made by ours.

We can change the future…because we can change today. We must not let any slip away and fade from the promise we are all born into so long as we are able. The difference is in you.

The future we are all destined to live will be fashioned by the hands of children…
The future our children are destined to fashion will be done so by your hands…

How will you create tomorrow?

~ Rachel ~

RACHEL WAS THE kind of 15-year-old who walked around with a sizable chip on her shoulder. She was in a constant state of revolt. I loved her and cared for her despite her anger and her petulance, but she was not the easiest person in the world to trust.

Rachel had been going head to toe with the law since she was twelve: shoplifting, drugs, truancy. With a girl like Rachel there were no easy life lessons because there were very few things that could penetrate the walls she had built.

Unbeknown to me, Rachel's probation officer – yes, she was a 15-year-old with the dubious distinction of her own probation officer – dropped her off at school one day last fall, watched her walk through the front entrance, and assumed he had fulfilled his appointed task regarding his itinerant charge. What he didn't see was that Rachel walked through the front door and straight out the back door and off campus. Unfortunately, this was not a case of a student playing hookey. Rachel's attendance at school was court-ordered. Skipping school for a student in her situation was a serious offense.

The next day, Rachel's absenteeism became my problem. She blamed her mother. "She couldn't bring me," she said. "My uncle was in a car wreck, and she had to see about him."

Rachel was a seasoned liar. She figured correctly that I didn't know about her probation officer, but what she didn't expect was the fact that Ms. Goforth wasn't about to accept her explanation without doing a little digging. "Fine," I said. "Let's give your mother a call so we can get your absence excused."

Rachel's discomfort was a dead give-away. When I got her mother on the phone, she explained the matter, saying, "After Rachel cussed me up one side and down the other, I said to hell with it and told her probation officer to drop her back off at school."

I didn't give Rachel a chance to deny it. I called her probation officer, and he was quick to confirm the mother's story. While I had him on the phone, I told him I was going to file contempt of court charges against Rachel. "I just want to give you a head's up," I said to him.

Rachel stood there fuming. When I hung up the phone, she lit into me with a string of expletives so foul that my only option was to ride it out. Before she could fill her lungs and start in again, I said, "You're the one who chose not to come to school, Rachel. You're responsible, not me. And not your mother or your probation office or the man in the moon either. You."

Rachel started hollering again, and I used my walkie-talkie to alert the vice-principal. I told Rachel I thought she needed to go back to class, but she refused.

"No way. I'm not going. You can't make me."

The verbal harangue escalated. The cussing and screaming continued after the vice-principal entered my office. I tried to tell Rachel that she was digging herself deeper and deeper into trouble, but by then the vice-principal had called for the campus police.

"You have two choices," the vice-principal said. "You can get your backpack and head over to ISS (In-School Suspension). Or you can keep this up and do it the hard way."

By now, street-wise Rachel understood what the "hard way" meant, so she stood up, looped her backpack over her shoulder, and allowed the police to escort her to ISS. "Good decision," the vice-principal said.

This, I decided, was proving to be a red-letter day if ever there was one.

When they were gone, I called Rachel's probation officer. I knew what Rachel was afraid of; she was afraid of being sent back to jail. Who wouldn't be? Her probation officer and I discussed this, and he assured me that this wasn't going to happen. "She has to step over the line a few more times before we send her back, Ms. Goforth. It can still happen, however. It's up to her."

"Do I have your permission to tell her what you just told me?" I asked him.

"Sure you do," he answered.

I decided to give Rachel a few hours to settle down before paying a visit to the ISS. This was an important moment, an opportunity to offer guidance without forcing Rachel's hand.

I escorted her to an empty conference room. We sat down. She was calmer now, but scared. I said, "Tell me something, Rachel. Tell me what your biggest fear is?"

I already knew the answer, of course, but I needed her to verbalize it.

"Goin' to juvenile TYC," she murmured, tears welling in her eyes. Prison.

"Okay. But I just talked to your probation officer, and that's not going to happen," I said. "You made a very bad choice, Rachel. And there will be consequences. You know that. But for now, you're not going to be sent to Juvenile TYC."

Rachel fell apart when she heard this, crying, sobbing, and apologizing through the tears. "I'm so sorry, Ms. Goforth. I'm so sorry."

Here was a teachable moment staring me in the face. "Now I understand what you are going through, but that is no excuse for talking to me the way you did. I didn't deserve it."

"I know."

I also wanted her to understand that what was done was done. Holding a grudge was not something I would ever do, and I didn't want her to walk away thinking we weren't in this together. We were.

Rachel and I talked for another 15 minutes about problem-solving and anger management and relationships. She was receptive. I think she was just scared enough to see the crossroads she was facing. Then I said, "And one other thing. I don't think your mom deserved the tongue-lashing you gave her. And I know the vice-principal certainly didn't deserve it."

"I know," she said again.

"Then maybe you should tell him." I had noticed that the vice-principal was on hall duty, so I waved him into the room. "Rachel's doing better," I said. I couldn't make Rachel apologize; that had to be her decision for it to have any real value. So I was hoping she would take her cue and speak up, and she did.

"I'm really sorry, Sir," she said. "I was wrong. I'm going to do better."

I couldn't have scripted a more appropriate response. And Rachel was sincere; I could hear it in her voice and so could vice-principal.

"I appreciate that, Rachel," he said. "I was going to have you sent over to Off-Campus Suspension for 15 days, but I don't think we'll do that now. Let's spend a week in ISS and then get you back to your classroom. How does that sound?"

"It sounds good. Thank you," she said. "I'm going to do better."

When the vice-principal was gone, I said, "You did well, Rachel. You made a mistake, and you owned up to it. And you accepted the consequences. That's the way the world works. And you can be successful out there if you put your mind to it. I know you can. I'm proud of you."

Rachel proved true to her word. She did do better. Her focus at school changed, and her grades improved. Suddenly attendance was no longer an issue. She fulfilled the conditions of her probation. When we passed in the hall, she smiled. That was reward enough for me. And, of course, I just had to tell her what an amazing smile it was.

~ Campus Parent ~

NO, IT IS not always possible to involve a parent in the process of educating a child. It's not always possible to have a parent involved in simply raising a child. I have seen many instances when a parent doesn't want to be there. We have all heard stories of men siring children and then abandoning them. We have all heard stories of women choosing drugs over the babies they carried in their wombs for nine months. But there are just as many parents who want to be there for their kids, but can't be.

She is the single mother working three jobs. He is the divorced father who sees his kids every other weekend.

She is doing everything she can to promote the survival of her family, but they still live in a two-room house in the projects. He works the night shift in a factory and doesn't return home until the kids are already at the bus stop.

She has no way of getting to a PTA meeting. He is just happy to keep the electricity on and food in the refrigerator.

If a parent isn't involved for whatever reason, does it mean we as educators are absolved of the responsibility? Of course not! We have to do what we can to meet their children's needs. It takes an entire school district to truly educate a child: teachers and counselors, administrators and staff people, bus drivers and custodians. We all have a responsibility to become, in essence, "campus parents" providing some measure of support for the "parentless" ones. It's one of the first things I tell a child when he or she steps into my office: "I'm your new school mom. And I'm going to shadow you until you get it right."

I have been in education for 27 years. Twenty-four of those years were spent in the classroom. While I have more certificates than you could possibly want to hear about, I am currently the At-Risk Coordinator at Central Freshman campus in San Angelo, Texas, a town of ninety thousand. Most of the experiences that shape the attributes that I discuss in this book occurred during those classroom years. These last three years working primarily with at-risk kids have allowed me to fine-tune those attributes.

The kids, as I said, have half a dozen nicknames for me that I fully embrace. I have even been called Mama and Mom. This is usually a slip of the tongue by a slightly embarrassed boy or girl, but every time it happens, I swear his or her eyes seem to light up.

"It's okay," I tell them. "You've just paid me the highest compliment."

I could go on about the awards I have received or the degrees on my wall, but what means more to me than anything in the world, and the one thing I would like to be remembered for, is my love of children.

~ The Power of the Positive ~

NINETY PERCENT OF the time when a teacher picks up the phone to call a parent, the call has negative implications. The student has misbehaved, failed a class, missed another assignment, or skipped school all together.

When I was a full-time classroom teacher, I learned along the way that a positive phone call had extraordinary power. A call to a parent touting a student's good behavior, a passing grade, participation in class, or improved attendance had a remarkable ripple effect. It provided parents with an opportunity to pat their student on the back and share a proud moment. It motivated the student. And it left both the parent and the child feeling as if school was indeed a good thing.

There were many times when I would call a parent just to say what a pleasure it was having their son or daughter in my class every day. You have no idea how surprised and pleased a mother or father would be when they heard me say, "I just wanted to call and tell you how much I enjoy your child," or "What a wonderful student you have. Thank you for sharing her with me."

It was like a ray of sunshine breaking through a cloudy day. Everyone benefited. I felt better about myself as a teacher. The parents had a reason to celebrate. And the student's value was validated.

I made a conscious decision years back to make more positive calls to parents than negative ones. It was a simple equation I tracked very closely. I would take it a step further and tell my students on the first day of class that they could expect me to inform them ahead of time if I intended to make a negative call. I thought this was only fair. The "good news" calls, however, would be a surprise, and they always were.

I still do this today in my role as an At-Risk Coordinator. I am not trying to curry favor with parents. I'm not worried about whether a child likes me or not. In most cases, I am trying to build the momentum that comes with good behavior or positive feedback. In some cases, however, I use these positive calls to subvert troubling behavior. I have often called the parents of the most troublesome student and said, "I thought I'd call and tell you how wonderful your son is," or "I want you to know how special I think your daughter is."

Without exception, this type of message results in a positive change in behavior. It goes back to the power of acknowledging a child's worth and validating his or her potential.

Positive affirmations create positive change. If a child thinks, "Well, if Ms. Goforth believes I'm a good kid and a wonderful person, then maybe I am."

Guidance comes in many forms. A kind word, a pat on the back, and a firm handshake can be as influential as a sound piece of advice, a helping hand, or attaching consequences to actions both good and bad.

I don't know if there is anything more satisfying than watching a child grow and change in a positive way. I don't know if there is anything more rewarding than watching them put their best foot forward. I don't know if there is anything more dramatic than watching them make a difference in the world.

~ Direction ~

APRIL HAD THE kind of smile that simply warmed the heart. Her almond eyes would come to life, and the most beautiful dimples would grace her cheeks. But April was typical of at-risk kids when it came to evaluating her future. Anticipating the direction her life might take was, much like recognizing success, a foreign concept.

This is, in many respects, a socio-economic phenomenon. Kids from higher economic groups are simply more aware of planning. They are introduced to the idea of planning ahead at an early age, and they are encouraged to examine their lives with that plan in mind. They may see college in their future as early as the 6th or 7th grade, and they are aware of all the prerequisites involved in getting there.

April was typical of at-risk kids who are often aware only of the prerequisites involved in getting through the day in one piece and anticipating what the night might bring. I have to introduce them to the notion of a long-term future based upon goals and dreams, and the steps required in bringing them to fruition.

I am involved currently in a program based around this very concept. I was asked some time back to be the coordinator at the ninth-grade level for the Angelo State University Mother-Daughter Program, a wonderful program designed to encourage girls to pursue a college education. Because ninth grade is the entry-level phase of the program, it is my privilege to select 30 girls every year who, if all goes well, will be the first generation of their families to attend college, with, of course, their mother's blessing and urging. April was one of the first girls to participate.

The program focuses on specific skills such as goal setting, leadership, and test taking as well as more general life skills such as embracing responsibility and matching consequences with actions. Perhaps the most important lesson of all is the gratification that comes from giving back to the community.

The program hinges upon the enthusiasm of both daughter and mother. It is a sad fact that there are many parents who don't encourage their kids in their academic pursuits, who make no demands on their academic performance, and who have no interest in whether or not their kids graduate from high school, much less matriculate at a higher level. While most of us want our children to prosper in areas we may not have, and attain what we may only have dreamed of, there are many parents who adopt a considerably different attitude, saying in essence, "Why should they (their children) have what we don't have? If an eighth-grade education is good enough for me…" You get the picture.

Not so for the mothers supporting the ASU Mother-Daughter Program. They have high expectations for their daughters and want them to achieve far beyond what they have achieved, to pursue careers that may never have been available to them, and to shoot for the stars.

Angelo State University assigns each girl a mentor. They provide each girl with an activity card that allows them to experience life on a college campus. Most importantly, the program plants a seed about the benefits of higher education. The school also assists the girls in pre-ACT and pre-SAT preparation, lends a hand in the application process, and guides them toward any scholarship benefits that might be available.

I am proud of the program. I was a first-generation college graduate. I understand the importance of higher education, the opportunities it brings, and the doors it opens. Would I be here today teaching and counseling kids without my degree? Almost certainly not! The guidance I received early in my life led to the belief that I could shoot for the stars. I can only hope that the guidance I am providing now will have the same effect.

A "keeper of hope" guides by example. We don't force a child down a path of our choosing. We help them find their own path, one with potential, one that challenges them and enlivens their spirit, one that opens the door to a fulfilling, rich life.

~ CHAPTER NINE ~
A Keeper of Hope Demonstrates a POSITIVE ATTITUDE

WHERE DOES A positive attitude begin? How does it develop? How does a teacher, mentor, or friend plant that seed?

For me, it begins by searching for the positive in every child. It begins by believing in them, encouraging them, caring about them, and loving them.

It is the absolute responsibility of all educators to find that positive "something" in even the most troubled or truculent child. It doesn't matter how deeply you have to dig; you have to find it.

It could be the way they smile, the sureness of their step, the sound of their laughter, or a hint of eye contact. Sometimes you might spend an entire semester mining for that positive "something," but when you unearth it, you have to cultivate it for all your worth.

It doesn't matter what a child's history is or what his or her records tells you. If you show them that you care, you can change that history. You can open new doors. You can create opportunity.

Last week a young man came into my office and took a seat across from me with a rap sheet longer than my arm. I didn't see his history as a reason to dismiss him as a hopeless cause. I saw his history as a reason to take action, to believe, encourage, care, and love him.

The search might try your patience or challenge your resolve, but my goal is to maintain a positive attitude throughout. The more positive my attitude is, the more likely I am going to elicit a positive response from my students.

So this chapter isn't just about their positive attitude, it's about yours and mine, as well.

~ Show Them You Care ~

THERE CAN BE nothing contrived about a demonstration of concern, compassion, or helpfulness. Caring comes with the territory. Sometimes it's complex, other times it's the simplest gesture in the world. If I see a kid without a coat on, and there are snowflakes in the air, I am compelled to say something. "Well, bless your heart, where's your coat?" If he's left it at home, we talk about planning better. If he says he doesn't own a coat, I put "finding Jason a coat" on my to-do list. If children are too embarrassed to apply for the free or reduced-cost meal program, I make sure they know how important their physical health is to me. That allows me to discuss their anxieties as well as their priorities.

If I know a student is facing a particularly tough test, I use every trick in the book to encourage and ignite his or her confidence. If I show my faith in them, they might just discover the added confidence it takes to get them over the hump.

~ I Just Want to be a Kid ~

SADLY, MANY KIDS have no concept of their self-worth.

Ask a child of 15 to list five positive qualities that make them special, and many stumble at one. "Okay then, what would your best friend say?" I ask.

"Well, I'm there if he needs me," Chris replied.

"Outstanding. So that's one. You're dependable. What about that amazing smile of yours? It makes me feel so good. So there's two. You're a neat kid. That's three. I'm a better person having known you. That's four." And so on. It's like priming the pump.

Chris was a prime example. He came to me while I was still a classroom teacher at Lee Junior High. He had just done a stretch at TYC, short for Texas Youth Commission. It wasn't his first time behind bars, and I could only hope it might be his last.

My last class of the day back then was called "School within a School." The class was popular with kids who had failed the previous year.

Chris was short for his age. Sad, dour eyes were his most conspicuous feature. He rarely spoke, and it took weeks to pry more than monosyllabic responses from him. I kept trying.

Every class period, I would invite one or two students up to my desk for a private chat. These chats incorporated almost every aspect of our starfish. I wanted my kids to know I was approachable; if they felt I was approachable, then recognizing my compassion came easily. If I could hold their attention in the midst of twenty-five other students, then I could demonstrate both the art of communicating and the art of listening. This individual attention was another way of acknowledging who they were and validating their self-worth. If they could experience my positive attitude in a one-on-one setting, then I felt sure they would feel comfortable seeking me out during the day or after school.

Mostly this was my way of getting to know them as individuals. The kids all knew I would be calling these sessions, and they knew they couldn't stonewall me. The gist of my "inquisition" was, in essence, "Tell me about yourself. Let me get to know you."

Chris was 15. He had been incarcerated, he told me, for breaking and entering. He was in youth prison for a year. He lived with his mother, a wheelchair-bound aunt, two little brothers, and two nephews. His mother worked nights, so Chris was in charge of dinner, getting the kids bathed and in bed, and tending his aunt. He was also in charge of homework and staying on top of six 9th grade classes.

Chris was expected to be responsible in ways that were well beyond his years. He didn't have a childhood. And that was his one wish.

The weight was unbearable. I could tell that just by watching his body language. My mantra with Chris was: "You're destined for great things. It's going to happen."

Two months later, Chris and two friends "tagged" the entire campus, spray-painting walls with gang lingo and expletives that shall go unnamed here. What was he thinking? Why in the world do such a thing to your own campus when the consequences are so dire? When I asked Chris that very question, he said, "I was just getting so tired of being responsible. At least in prison, I can have a room to myself and just be a 15-year-old for a while."

This is a remarkable and telling answer that suggests just how desperate Chris was. He had intentionally set himself up. I was confused because he had been doing well in school. I was dismayed because this young man was not able to see any other options, options most of us might take for granted. I was also angry because I had not been able to paint a clearer picture of those options. I may have made myself approachable. I may have felt as if I had communicated well with him, but apparently he wasn't ready or able to reciprocate.

I was sitting in my classroom shortly thereafter when the phone rang. A man identifying himself as Chris's lawyer asked if I would be willing to testify in court on Chris's behalf. "I know this is an unusual request," he said, "But when I asked Chris if there was anyone who believed in him, or if there was anyone who would speak up for him, he said, 'Ms. Goforth believes in me.' He said no one has had more of an impact on him than you, ma'am."

I was, to say the least, deeply moved. A child could hardly bestow a more meaningful reward upon an educator. I did in fact appear in court as a character witness for Chris. When I was asked under oath to give my opinion of him, I said, "He's an amazing young man who's never had a chance to be a kid. He carries a heavy load at home. I will say this; I expect great things out of Chris, and I will be waiting when he gets back."

Chris served his time. Will he ever discover that amazing side of himself, a side that is so apparent to me? Will he ever explore his potential to the fullest? He has a leg up, I think, knowing that someone else believes in him. That's a beginning. Now it's up to him. He has tasted a more positive view of life. He has seen that a positive attitude is not simply a façade. Are the negatives he has butted head with the more powerful forces? I don't know for certain, but I have to believe that facing the world every day with a negative attitude is a no-win situation. The burden is too great. But there is built-in energy in a positive attitude, and Chris strikes me as savvy enough to recognize this, if not today, then maybe tomorrow.

~ Mr. and Mrs. Lee ~

MEET MR. AND Mrs. Lee. Mid-sixties. More years of marriage than most of us have been alive. Life-long educators. Mr. Lee was my high school algebra teacher. Mrs. Lee taught English in the same building.

They both retired some years back after the kind of careers that make youngsters like me want to pursue teaching as a profession. That's a high compliment. They left their mark on many a student, and two of those students were responsible for saving Mr. Lee's life one evening.

Mr. Lee was puttering around the house that very inauspicious night when his heart went into cardiac arrest. Unfortunately, Mrs. Lee was out that night at her weekly bunko game at a friend's house. Mr. Lee had just enough life left in him to reach for the phone and dial 911.

The paramedics arrived some minutes later and calmly and efficiently went about the business of keeping Mr. Lee from breathing his last breath. One of the paramedics recognized their patient from days gone by. He bent over the gurney as they were rolling Mr. Lee toward the ambulance and said, "Mr. Lee. It's alright." When Mr. Lee heard his name, he opened his eyes. The paramedic smiled.

"Remember me? I had you for fifth period algebra. I wouldn't have made it through that class without your help," he said. Mr. Lee could hardly manage a nod. "I'll take care of you, Sir. Don't worry. Time for me to return the favor."

They rushed Mr. Lee to the hospital where he suffered two more attacks. By then, Mrs. Lee was pacing in the waiting room and frantic with worry. A doctor came out with a clipboard in his hand. He smiled warmly.

"Mrs. Lee, I'm Dr. Petry. Your husband is going to be fine."

"Oh, thank God. And thank you," she said.

"You don't remember me, do you?" the doctor said. "You got me through English class when I couldn't distinguish a predicate from a modifier. I won't ever forget it. And don't worry. I wasn't much good at English, but I'll make sure your husband gets the best of everything."

It may have been the wildest of coincidences that two of the Lee's former students were part of the team who tended to him that night, but it was no coincidence that the paramedic remembered Mr. Lee, or that Dr. Petry remembered Mrs. Lee. They were the kind of teachers kids don't forget, dependable and caring, consistent and supportive. Teachers who held nothing back, who served as positive role models, and who sent kids home with more than just schoolwork. They sent them home with a sense of self and with life lessons that would last a lifetime.

Mr. and Mrs. Lee were not "sometime" teachers. They were there every day giving of themselves. Kids don't forget that. Like most of us, kids have long memories when it comes to people who give of themselves, people who genuinely contribute, and people who add color to the palette of life.

~ Reasons Why ~

TIMOTHY WAS A blonde, blue-eyed, young man who wore the exact same clothes to school every day, rain or shine, snow or sleet. This wasn't a fashion statement on Timothy's part; it was all he had. Timothy was so slight that a strong breeze would probably have knocked him over. On the other hand, he rarely missed a day of school or failed to turn in an assignment.

When the boy who sat next to Timothy in my computer class reported that a can of tuna was missing from his backpack, my first thought was: "Why in the world would anyone steal a can of tuna?"

We pulled several kids out of class, including Timothy. When we asked him to open his backpack, the empty tuna can tumbled out.

Timothy made no effort to deny what he had done. "I took it," he admitted. "I'm sorry, but I haven't eaten anything in three days."

Three days! At it turned out, Timothy's parents had failed to sign Timothy up for the free meal program because they couldn't read. This happened all the time. An association with the free meal program was like walking into school wearing a billboard that read: "We're poor, and we're uneducated."

Timothy may have been in my computer class, but the computer was the last thing on his mind. How do I respond to that? I had come to school that morning after sleeping in a warm bed, eating a filling breakfast, and bundling up in a sweater and coat. Do I discipline Timothy? Do I leave scars of love, or scars of hurt? Do I add to his woes, or do I try and add a measure of worth to his life? Do I value his existence, or do I devalue it even more than it already is? I have a choice. But his only choice was to survive.

Why do I include Timothy under the section dedicated to maintaining a positive attitude on my own behalf and instilling a similar attitude in the children I see? Timothy doesn't need my sympathy. His burden is heavy enough. He needs my energy. He needs options that might just allow him to step beyond a life where starvation seems to be a very real possibility. He needs hope, and the best vehicle for instilling hope is to take action. Taking action is a means of creating new experiences, and experience is what we use to change our view of the world. And Timothy's view of the world was in dire need of change.

~ The Gift ~

WORKING WITH CHILDREN and young adults is truly a gift. It is something I feel in my heart. It is not something I planned, however. It is, I have decided, a gift from above, a talent given to me by God. Thankfully this heartfelt gift led me into education.

One thing that I discovered early in my career, when I was both a classroom teacher and a foster parent, is that kids are hungry for love. If they don't find it at home or within a family unit, the concept of self-love is probably foreign to them. And even if there is a parent at home who loves them, they will still often search for love in places that you and I recognize as traps; they may understand how slim the odds are in many of the relationships they pursue, but the need for love is a powerful force. I have seen many young girls accept an "unwanted pregnancy" for that very reason: their maternal instincts tell them that a child will love them regardless, and that they will love that child with equal fervor. It is a way of quelling the hunger.

I had been an At-Risk Coordinator for only five days when a beautiful, petite seventh-grader named Vickie came into my office and introduced herself by saying, "I hear you help people."

I guess the word had gotten around. "I sure do," I said in reply. "Why don't you sit down?"

Vickie had an angelic quality to her. It may have been her satin hair or her golden skin, or it may have been the gentleness of her gaze or the sweetness of her smile.

"I think I have a problem," she began. It was not a completely original line, but neither was my reply.

I said, "Why do you think that?"

"I did a home pregnancy test. It came back positive."

I wanted to ask her what in the world a seventh-grader was doing having sex in the first place, but I knew better than to ask a question like that. "Have you told your mother?"

"No. I'm afraid to. She'll kill me."

"We have to tell your mother, Vickie. This is important and very serious. This is a baby we're discussing now, okay?" Firm but gentle. This was a case of building trust in a big hurry. "We have to get you to a doctor. We have to start thinking about nutrition for you and about your baby's health."

"I know. I'll tell her. But can't you give me a couple of days? Please?" Her anxiety level was huge, but it was also important to set limits.

"I'll give you two days, Vickie."

Two days passed, and I called her in. No, she had not told her mother. I placed the call then and there and invited her mother in for a visit. Vickie was already in tears by the time her mother arrived and begging me to explain the situation. I did, and her mother went off. I heard her say what most mothers would probably say in a similar situation. "I can't believe you did this. Why didn't you talk to me? We could have gotten you started on the pill."

It wasn't, I was soon to learn, all that simple. The mother had also been pregnant herself at 14. A sister had just given birth. Then I found out that Vickie's boyfriend, a boy two years her senior, actually lived with the family. These were the cards Vickie had been dealt.

Fortunately the pregnancy turned out to be a false alarm, but rumors some months later that Vickie had been physically abused motivated me to call her in again. Her coat, I noticed, was buttoned high on her neck. I began by saying, "Hey girl, how are you doing?"

"All right."

"I heard something I think we should talk about."

"I had a fight with my mom."

"I heard something else, Vickie." I didn't tell her that one of her best friends had been in to see me. "I need you to take your coat off, sweetheart."

Eventually I coaxed her out of her coat, and the bruises were everywhere. There was even a man's handprint around her neck. All I could say was, "Oh, Vickie."

"But he loves me," she said, wanting to believe it so badly.

"No, Vickie. He doesn't love you. No one who loves you would ever do such a thing to you. Ever. And we need to report this right now."

"No, Ms. Goforth. No. I don't want him to leave me." Her desperation was palpable; it filled the room. "He really does love me."

"No," I said again. But she would never believe it. She needed to be loved. Wanted to be loved. We did report the incident, but I knew she would recant her accusation in court. Her mother arrived, and we hugged. "We've had a long, tough year, haven't we, Ms. Goforth?" she said, without much hope.

"Yes, we have," I said. "But we'll get through it. As long as we have each other."

The boyfriend moved out eventually, and Vickie's family moved away. I lost track of her. But I learned something valuable from my interaction with Vickie. I can't hold on to them. As much as I might want to, I have to let go. Sometimes all I can do is help them up, dust them off, and send them on their way.

~ Johnny and the $12.00 Art Kit ~

NEVER UNDERESTIMATE THE impact you might have on a child. Never question the effect your positive attitude can have. Whenever I question myself, I think of Johnny.

Johnny is a wonderful example of how much a teachable moment can mean to a child.

Johnny was a sight to behold as he walked across campus or down the hall. He was as thin as a beanpole and just as tall. He had stringy, raven-black hair that he slicked back off his forehead. Johnny was constantly in trouble because his pants were several sizes too big, and they hung so far below his waist that his cheeks were permanently on display. "Sagging," as they called it, was not an acceptable fashion statement in the public school system, at least not to the degree that Johnny took it.

I finally confronted him. "Either get a belt and pull your pants up or get a pair that fits."

"I don't have a belt. And this is the only pair I have," he admitted. "They're hand-me-downs from my brothers."

Johnny wasn't being coy or flippant. He was stating the facts. So that very day I snuck out to the local department store and bought a new pair of jeans and a belt and had them delivered in Johnny's name to the front office.

The next day, he showed up for class in his new jeans and belt, and they fit perfectly. He came up to me and said, "They look great, don't they? Thank you, Ms. G."

"I don't know what you're talking about, Johnny," I said in an even voice.

He just smiled. He walked back to his desk. His step was a little more sure, and his shoulders were a little straighter. He was right; the jeans looked darned good.

Unfortunately Johnny was a slow learner. He could take an entire day on one math problem and still get it wrong. He could hardly write, and his reading skills were abysmal. It wasn't a lack of effort; it was a lack of understanding.

But what he could do was draw. He was one of the most gifted sketch artists I had ever seen, and the pleasure he took from creating a landscape or a still-life was immeasurable. He was equally as skilled at calligraphy. Where he had learned it, I never knew for sure. Johnny was deep into the gangs, and the gangs liked to use calligraphy and Chinese characters in their tattoos.

Johnny practiced his calligraphy using ordinary pencils and crayons. He didn't have enough money for brushes or ink. So the last six weeks of the semester, I pulled him aside and offered him a challenge.

"If you pass one class this six weeks, I promise to surprise you with something special." One class. It may sound insignificant to most of us, but Johnny hadn't passed a class all year. I was willing to try anything, even a little bribery.

Lo and behold, it happened. He scored a 71 in English and passed the class by one point. Time to make good on my promise. I went to the arts and crafts store the next day and bought him an art kit. I got lucky. It was on sale. The kit contained colored pencils, charcoals, and pastels. It came with a set of calligraphy pens and two drawing pads.

When I saw the look on Johnny's face, you would have thought I had worked a miracle on his behalf. That simple art kit meant the world to him. He guarded it with his life. He carried it everywhere. Periodically he would drop a drawing off at my office or write my name in Chinese characters.

"This is wonderful," he must have said to me a dozen times, and it occurred to me that he had probably never received a gift that hadn't been previously owned by someone else.

Several years passed. I lost touch with Johnny, but I had my drawings to remind me of him. One day, rumors of a drug bust filtered through the school. Gunfire had left one young man dead. Johnny. My Johnny. His gang ties had finally caught up with him. I felt horrible.

Another ten years passed. I happened to go into a sandwich shop on my way home from work, and the young lady behind the counter apparently recognized me.

"Excuse me," she said. "But you're Ms. Goforth, aren't you?"

"Yes, I am. How did you know that?" I asked. "Did I have you in class?"

"No, ma'am. You had my best friend in one of your classes."

"Really? Who was that?"

"Johnny. Johnny Isley."

"Oh my! Johnny."

We talked about Johnny for several minutes, and then she said, "I have something of Johnny's."

"Something of Johnny's? What do you mean?"

"Do you remember the art kit you gave him?"

"I sure do."

"After he died, I asked his mom if I could have it. You know, something to remember him by. I keep it on a shelf in my apartment. It was the most sacred thing he had, Ms. Goforth."

A $12.00 art kit! That something so simple could mean so much to a young man – and then to his best friend – reminded me that we can alter a life just by caring. We can bring meaning to a life just by reaching out.

It also reminded me that being a "keeper of hope" is not a passive thing. It calls for a positive attitude. It requires us to take action. We may not always see the results, but there would be no results at all if we did nothing.

~ CHAPTER TEN ~

A Keeper of Hope Must Be DEPENDABLE

BEING DEPENDABLE IN the eyes of a 15-year-old ninth-grader runs pretty true to the definition we all associate with the word.

A dependable person is someone you can rely on, someone you can trust, and someone who is there when you need them. Easier said than done.

A dependable educator will always be there. A "sometime" teacher won't do. A "sometime" mentor has nothing concrete to share. And a "sometime" friend isn't a friend at all.

Fifteen is a fragile age, and consistency is a must. But consistency doesn't discriminate about age. We all want consistent, dependable people in our lives. Consistency, dependability, and trust are all woven of the same cloth. They all demonstrate respect, and the kids I see every day are starved for respect. Often times the simplest way to show respect is to do exactly what I say I'm going to do.

This is not a "sometime" proposition. My kids have to be able to count on me any time of day. If I say I'm going to do something, it's incumbent upon me to follow through. With kids, making a commitment is the fastest way I know of finding yourself under the microscope.

The rule of thumb is simple. Never promise what you can't deliver. Never promote your dependability if you can't deliver the goods. It could be something as simple as a promise of school supplies, like a spiral notebook or a box of note cards. If I show up at school the next day without that spiral notebook, I lose value in the eyes of every student who knows about it. These are kids who wear their distrust like a shroud; it's all they've ever known. If they have parents, they generally find themselves well down on Mom and Dad's priority list. They resist authority, mistrust the police, and have little faith in society as a whole. They have spent a good amount of their childhoods living with, and expecting, broken promises. It's not a great way to grow up.

Even if I show up a day later with that spiral notebook, the damage is done. This is not a matter of sympathy, but rather one of empathy. It's not a matter of enabling, rather one of educating.

I am nothing if not consistent, and it has nothing to do with garnering favor. If I tell a student I'm writing him or her up for missing an assignment or for skipping class, it's never an empty threat. They have to know that consistency and dependability work both ways. Life is a two-way street. The good with the bad. There is as much to be gained from delivering the notebook I promised as there is in following through on a disciplinary matter.

If I tell one of our basketball players that I'm going to show up for one of his games, I show up as promised. If a girl in our choir is expecting me to attend a recital, her recital is on my "can't miss" list.

Most of my kids would rather the principal call their parents with a disciplinary matter rather than sending them to me. "Call my mother if you want, but please don't call Ms. Goforth."

As surprising as this may sound, I take this as a compliment. At home, they expect to be scolded. The hollering and screaming they encounter is such a commonplace event that it rolls off their backs like water down a slide. In their experience, hollering and screaming over matters regarding school performance, or school-related behavioral issues, generally is more show than substance. Most of my kids would tell you that if their parents truly cared, they might care, too. That's the difference. With me, there's no place to hide. They know I care. They know I have very real expectations for them as students and as human beings. They know we have established a relationship built on respect and dependability, and that the nature of that relationship requires accountability.

Knowing how ineffective hollering and screaming is, I almost never raise my voice. And when I'm disappointed, I lower my voice even further. This subdued tone draws them in. It reinforces my sincerity. So when I say, "I really expected more from you," it hits home.

As I've said, this is the nature of the relationship I try so diligently to establish with my students. The goal is the sharing of mutual respect. When a child knows someone loves them the way I do, he or she does not want to disappoint. That desire to be true to a relationship is also a growing sign of self-respect. Kids are no different than you or I; they recognize their mistakes. Try as they might, they can't hide from them. But they must also understand that I don't think any less of them because they might have slipped up. Who among us doesn't? The message I try to convey to my kids is that it is the response to the mistake that counts most.

That's the beauty of dependability. It is a two-way street, which is why it is such a positive teaching tool.

~ Heather ~

MOST KIDS SPEND a maximum of 45 days at the district's alternative school before returning to their home campus. Heather had spent three solid years there. To look at her, you would never suspect it. She was petite, funny, and charming. She was also sassy, undisciplined, and insecure.

When she finally arrived at the Central Freshman campus, she was immediately assigned to my credit recovery lab. But fixing a failing grade implies an interest in passing, and Heather had no concept of the future beyond the next 15 or 20 minutes of her life. Our first day didn't go well. Heather talked non-stop the entire period.

I suggested she pay me a visit after class. When I tried to explain the basics of classroom behavior and the rules surrounding mandatory detention, Heather exploded. She filled the room with a litany of four-letter words and the use of the F-word. In the state of Texas, using the F-word is grounds for an educator to file a citizen's complaint, and every student knows that, Heather included. I told her, before she stomped out of the room, that I would be notifying the office. Like I said, not a good first day.

While I may have had a choice in the matter of filing the complaint, kids still have to understand the rules of cause and affect, and they have to recognize that every action comes with a consequence.

When I arrived at the office, Heather was there. She informed me that her mother was on the way up, as well. She said it in that "just you wait" voice that every teacher has heard a hundred times.

By this time, the police had already started filling out the paper-work for the citizen's complaint, which carries a mandatory court appearance and a $300 fine. All that was lacking was my signature. The penalty may sound harsh, but so many kids come to school believing the F-word is part of the vernacular, and that if it's good enough for home or for the streets then it should be good enough for school and work, and the only way to break the habit is by fighting fire with fire.

Heather's plan backfired. Her mother and I, as it turned out, had known each other for years, so she didn't turn out to be the fire-breathing dragon that Heather had hoped for. In fact, she was very supportive of me and my handling of the situation.

Both the on-duty police officer and my principal came to my defense, as well, but they did it without putting Heather on the defense. Principal Frazier said, "If anyone in this school is in your corner, Heather, I think we all know it's Ms. Goforth."

"I've worked with Ms. G for a lot of years," the police officer said, "And I've never heard a mean or rude thing come out of her mouth."

"I know that," Heather said. "And I shouldn't have said what I said. I didn't mean it."

"Do you think you can abide by the rules in the A+ lab, Heather?" I asked her. "And take care of your business the way I know you can?"

"Yes," she said. "I can. And I will."

"Well, in that case, I won't be filing charges," I said to the police officer. I shredded the ticket. "Heather and I will take it from here."

This was a teachable moment, as I call them. When the principal and the police officer were gone, I said, "Heather, what happened this afternoon happened. It was a learning experience, and I want you to see it that way. From this moment on, everything is fine between us. And we're going to work our backsides off to get you your credits. Okay?"

"Okay."

Was I wrong to shred up that ticket? I don't think so. I believe that kids deserve a second chance. Taking advantage of a second chance is a learning experience. It allows a child to see the world in a different light. Life lessons come in many different forms, and sometimes the hardest part of being a teacher or counselor, or just an adult reaching out to a kid, is which lesson makes the most sense at any given time.

I will go out of my way to defend a child's right to learn. That is the bottom line for me. It doesn't matter who the child is or what his or her circumstances are. Every child deserves the opportunity.

~ Jekyll and Hyde ~

DEMONSTRATING CONSISTENCY AND dependability doesn't imply perfection; that's the good news. The better news is that kids aren't expecting perfection.

Yes, if I say "Good morning, Sunshine," to a student in the morning, then I think it's important that I offer a "Have a great day," in the afternoon. Kids deserve that consistent energy on my part. However, that doesn't suggest that the positive energy is there every waking moment. That would not be realistic. After all, there is a little bit of Dr. Jekyll and Mr. Hyde in all of us. When that positive energy is not there, I've learned to step away. My issues should not become their issues. That's not the job of a 15-year-old. On the other hand, this does not preclude the sharing of an empathetic moment with a child when the time is right. Allowing them to see that hard times are a part of every adult's life can and should be a positive life lesson. In my role as an educator, I would not be painting a fair picture if my kids thought my life was all a bed of roses.

The messages are clear. Hard times are not the end of the world. Hard times create opportunity. We can rise above hard times and remain consistent to our beliefs. Hard times are not an excuse for being undependable or untrustworthy.

~ The Payoff ~

MANY OF THE young men and women I associate with at the Central Freshman campus have seen more than their share of life's unpleasant side. So what do they do? They build walls to protect themselves. The walls inevitably come with a certain degree of cynicism. In the cynical part of their minds there is a flashing neon sign that says no one does anything without a payoff. They assume that everyone has an ulterior motive.

It's not at all unusual for a student to say, "Why do you care? What's in it for you?" In other words, why be nice? Why be empathetic? Why give a damn? What's the payoff?

My answer: "Because I'm supposed to."

"How do you know you're supposed to, Ms. Goforth?"

"Because I can feel it in my heart."

I think most of the kids I meet can sense my sincerity. It's hard to fake. I think most of them discover fairly quickly that what they see is what they get. Ironically that's all they want: consistency, dependability. And not just from me. From their parents, their friends, their teachers. And from my perspective, that's not too much to ask.

~ Samantha ~

SAMANTHA IS A wonderful example of how interconnected validation and consistency really are. They are, by necessity, perfect bedfellows.

Validating children one day and leaving them adrift the next does more damage than ignoring them altogether.

The odds were stacked against Samantha from the very beginning. She never knew her father. Her mother was a recovering drug addict and was under house arrest at the time. On the other hand, Samantha was smarter than her performance in school implied. She had failed 9th grade as a 15-year-old and had returned again as a 16-year-old. This was her last chance.

She and I discussed her situation at the beginning of the year, and I could see how badly Samantha wanted to be with her friends at Central High. I assured her that she could spend her second semester at Central if she could accrue an appropriate number of credits over the next 12 weeks.

Samantha's eyes lit up. Suddenly she had a goal. Suddenly she was motivated. And for the first six or eight weeks, she worked her little heart out. She was passing her classes and demonstrating a growing maturity toward her homework. I was genuinely hopeful. And I could tell that she was hopeful, as well.

It didn't last.

One day she lost her temper in art class. It was not a pretty sight. You don't go off on a teacher without serious consequences. She received ISS: In-School Suspension. It happened again in history class, and the teacher invited Samantha to leave. The third incident occurred two days later, in the credit recovery lab, when Samantha challenged the class seating arrangement. The teacher responded by sending Samantha to the vice-principal's office.

Something was dreadfully wrong. This was not the Samantha I had been working with for the last eight weeks. Something was setting her off, and it wasn't an art assignment or a seating chart. I went to our vice-principal and intervened. "We need to get to the bottom of this," I told him. "Samantha isn't like this. And she's been doing so well."

He agreed.

I invited Samantha to take a walk, and we ended up at a table in the common area.

"I know you, Samantha. I know how special you are," I said to her.

"And these outbursts just aren't like you at all. Talk to me. Tell Ms. Goforth what's going on. Let's clear the air."

Samantha, God love her, couldn't hold back the tears. And I was praying she wouldn't. They spilled over and turned into sobbing. She tried talking. "I'm not going to make it to Central (the high school). I'm not going to make it, Ms. G." A show of tears, as I said earlier, is a good thing. Once I see tears, I know there is hope. Tears are an expression of how badly a child's heart is hurting, and Samantha was most certainly hurting. I let her cry. Crying is like a bottle full of hurt overflowing. The bottle needs to be emptied periodically. "I am trying so hard, and my mom keeps telling me how great my brothers are and how smart they are, and that I'm never going to make it. And she's right."

When the tears slowed, I said, "First of all, you are going to make it. How do I know? Because I've seen the kind of work you can do. And second of all, you let me worry about whether or not you're passing."

We talked about the frustration she was feeling. We talked about the inappropriate way she was handling her frustration. And we also talked about anger and misplaced anger.

I went a step further. I brought Samantha's credit recovery teacher to the table. We discussed Samantha's dilemma and her mind-set. My fellow teacher was shocked. "I had no idea," he admitted. "But we'll get you through this. We'll all work together."

All at once, an adversary was an ally. Samantha got a taste of how important open and honest communication was. She got a taste of how important teamwork and trust were. I hugged her, and she hugged me, and then she got back to work. We used her deteriorating situation as a learning experience, and that learning experience became a launch pad that saw her advance the following semester to Central High.

~ A Knot in the Rope ~

LIFE FOR MANY a child is like a rope. The rope has to be climbed. In some cases, the rope is slippery and dangerous, and just hanging on is a huge effort. I do what I can to halt the skid. We all do. No one wants to see a child hanging by a thread and hopeless to find his or her way to the top. I see myself as a knot at the end of the rope. I suppose most educators see themselves in the same light, as well. Parenting can be that way in some cases too. I can help them hang on, and I can point the way back up, but I cannot force them to climb.

Kids want intervention. They want interaction. Despite signals that might suggest otherwise, they want someone to tie a knot in the rope from which they're dangling. They do, sometimes desperately. But at times they get tired of hanging on, despite my support, or that of any "keeper of hope."

If a kid goes back home and his parents are selling drugs or his family is living under a bridge or his guardian is just simply disconnected, it's like struggling against the tide.

If the cupboards are bare and the refrigerator is empty, the temptation to steal is overwhelming. Gangs offer camaraderie and a sense of belonging, if not true friendship. Poverty can be an unstoppable force, and survival sometimes doesn't distinguish between good and bad.

Kids want structure in their lives. They want order and direction despite the mixed messages that teachers and parents, mentors, and counselors often encounter. If their lives at home don't provide that structure, then they come to school with the same hope, even if that hope is subconscious or unspoken.

Some years back, I was reassigned from history class to a newly created computer lab. Most notable about the history class was a troublesome girl who was so starved for discipline and structure that she would intentionally disrupt the class, forcing me to reprimand her and, when appropriate, ship her off to detention.

Shortly after changing classes, this same young lady cornered me after school and requested with total sincerity that I yell at her. Or, as she put it, "Come down hard on me. Really get on me!"

I was naturally incredulous and said, "What in the world are you talking about?"

"The teacher we have in history now just lets us run all over him. I miss you. I just want you to yell at me once, 'Sit down, Shelly. Get your paper out and close your mouth!' Because when you got on me, I knew you cared."

She was dead serious. The structure and discipline that had been imposed upon her and the class was no longer there, and she missed it. She was actually starved for it.

Kids test the rules, just like they test an adult's meddle, but that is not to dismiss the need for order in their lives. Boundaries, limits, and guidelines are all forms of order that kids might fight, resent, or challenge, but having no structure or order is far more debilitating.

~ Philip ~

THE CENTRAL FRESHMAN campus is associated with an alternative school for short-term or long-term disciplinary placement. The school is named Carver. Unfortunately there is never an enrollment shortage at Carver. The minimum assignment is fifteen days. The campus is within walking distance of Central Freshman and draws on kids from all over the district.

Because a student who is serving a 15-day term at Carver is still officially enrolled in school, one of my regular duties, in the past, was to visit the facility on a regular basis and disperse homework assignments.

Philip was an alternative school kid. When he wasn't serving time there, he was an eighth-grader at Lee Junior High, which meant he was destined for the Central Freshman campus if he could work his way through alternative school and then pass the rest of his classes.

One day, I walked through the doors of Carver only to find that Philip was the most frustrated kid in the building. I introduced myself. We started talking. By the time our conversation got around to school, I found out rather quickly that the source of Philip's frustration was a rather baffling math assignment.

I offered my help. When we were done with the assignment, I struck up a conversation. After a while, I went into my campus-parent mode and said, "When you get to Central, I'm expecting big things from you, Philip. Do you hear me? I'm expecting you to set an example for the rest of the kids with your behavior. And I'm expecting you to be in class every day and to do the work. If you don't, I'm going to pull your ears off. Got it?"

"Yes, ma'am. I got it."

I didn't recognize Philip when he showed up at Central the following year. He had grown and filled out. His hair was shorter. Four weeks into the term, he sought me out. "Remember me?" he said. "We met at Carver last year, and you said you'd pull my ears off if I didn't take care of my business."

"Philip. Of course." I finally placed the face and had to chuckle. "And have you been taking care of business?"

"Yes, ma'am. Every day."

"Good for you. I knew you could do it." This called for a hug.

It was an amazing thing. Fifteen minutes of personalized attention had stayed with Philip all year. Fifteen minutes of validating him as a worthwhile young man and nudging him a little closer to the light.

~ A Difference Maker ~

THERE IS A quote that is often attributed to Ralph Waldo Emerson that reads: "To leave the world a bit better, whether by a healthy child, a garden patch, or a redeemed social condition; to know even one life has breathed a little easier because you have lived. This is to have succeeded."

As a "keeper of hope," the words go a long way toward spelling out my definition of success.

It is true that I would hope to make a positive difference in the life of every child I touch. Who among us doesn't feel that way? A teacher may serve a different need than a mentor, and a parent may have different responsibilities than a friend, but the bottom line is the same. We all hope our influence promotes a positive outcome in the life of a child.

The beauty of what I do every day in my role as an At-Risk coordinator – and this is surely something every teacher and parent can relate to – is that the kids I work with are difference-makers in my life. It's been 27 years since I began my teaching career, and I can still recall every classroom and most of the faces. I can still picture their smiles, and I can still see the twinkle of expectation in their eyes. I can remember the struggles right along side the triumphs. I can see the tears and hear the laughter. And while I may have left scars of love on them – because love is never simple and rarely easy – they have all left scars of love on me, as well. I am a better person for it. I can only hope that my influence has been as meaningful.

I found the key nearly 27 years ago when I quit teaching this subject or that subject and began teaching children. The moment I stepped away from the curriculum, I began building relationships. It's not so very different from that classic line in the movie Field of Dreams, "If you build it, he will come." If you build a relationship with a child, the education will come.

Earlier we shared another saying, "They don't care how much you know until they know how much you care." It bears repeating. Caring and loving spur all kinds of positive behavior. Kids don't mind being challenged if they know it comes out of love. Kids don't rebel against love. They don't rebel against someone who believes in them wholeheartedly. They want to do well, and they are looking for a reason to do well. Sometimes it's the job of an adult to inspire them.

Once a child knows you care, the sky is the limit.

~ CHAPTER ELEVEN ~

A Keeper of Hope is LOVE

IN THE BEGINNING of this book we talked about the starfish, and how it represents the many hats an effective educator wears. It represents the eleven attributes that have helped me to acknowledge and validate my kids, to make them feel good about themselves and their place in the world and, most importantly by far, to show them how much I care for them as people and individuals, not just as warm bodies. By now, it should be no surprise to find love at the center of our starfish, and it should be no surprise that the ten tools represented by the arms of the starfish mean very little if they don't lead to a willingness to love the kids in our care.

Eleanor Roosevelt described the mission of all "keepers of hope" when she said, "It's better to light a candle than to curse the darkness." Could any words paint a picture more apropos to the well-being of a child?

I never tire of telling my kids that I see myself as the luckiest person in the world: after all, I get paid to come to my particular institute of learning and get to love kids all day long. Yes, they may look at me like I'm crazy, but deep down, they understand. This is love for them as people, as individuals, and as worthwhile, relevant souls.

It begins the first day of the school year. It begins with a smile, a "Good morning," and a genuine sense of commitment and caring.

Then when I walk into a classroom, they way I did some weeks back, and I hear Robert call to me from the back of the room, "I love you, Ms. Goforth," it's just as natural as can be that I'm able to look back at him and say, "Right back at you, man."

The kids get it. This isn't physical love or romantic love, this is caring love. This is the kind of love that I bring to school every morning. This is the kind of genuine caring that people naturally pick up on. So when I'm sitting outside in the morning in my role as the "Good Morning Lady," and the two Down syndrome kids in our school run up and throw their arms around me, squeezing and saying, "I love you, Mama G," it's like magic; it's what gives meaning to my profession in all its glory. They know how glad I am to see them because I've been greeting them that way since the first day of school. I may not have them in class, but they still see me as approachable. They feel safe in expressing themselves. And just like you and I, they can sense genuine caring and a consistency of spirit that builds trust and predictability.

~ All You Need is Love ~

THERE IS NOTHING more powerful than love. If I can exhibit a caring, loving attitude toward the kids I encounter every day, the result can only be positive.

When I applied for my first At-Risk Coordinator position several years back, the question I answered with the most assurance and absolute confidence may have also been the simplest.

"What is the most powerful and most important characteristic of an At-Risk Coordinator?" I was asked.

"Love," I said, looking the interview panel straight in the eyes. And then I explained. "If I don't truly love these kids, I'm not going to be able to help them. When everyone else has given up on them, that's when they need it the most. If I'm not willing to put my heart on the line, I'll never be able to get to their hearts. And if I can't get to their hearts, the walls they've built will never come down."

An open heart is as important as an open mind. More so, in fact. It is absolutely essential that the kids see the real me, no strings attached, if I am to have any hope of opening their hearts and breaking through their walls.

It's not a matter of bargaining. Most of the kids I have encountered since that first interview believe without equivocation that they have nothing left to lose and very little to gain.

This willingness to approach my work with an open heart can be tricky when it comes to Debbie Goforth the person, and my personal life. This is about the students I counsel. This is about their lives and their futures, not mine. It's imperative that I keep my personal life separate from the business of teaching students and tending to their world. Yet sometimes it happens; sometimes I can't separate the two. One of my students – a little wisp of a girl – caught me with tears in my eyes the last time my dad was hospitalized. She waltzed right up to me and said, "Are you alright, Ms. Goforth? How come you're crying?"

There was never a question in my mind about sharing a personal moment with this young lady. On the one hand, she had reached out to me. To deny my feelings would have been an insult to the compassion she had offered me. On the other hand, sharing a small part of myself in this situation was an effective way of showing her that I have problems just like anyone else. Different in some ways, perhaps, but similar in others.

"My daddy's in the hospital," I told her. "And I'm just such a daddy's girl. I worry about him."

She hugged me. Just like that, she hugged me. Then she said, "If you need me, I'm here, Ms. Goforth. Count on it."

"Thank you, sweetheart. I know you are," I told her. "And that makes it so much easier."

It wasn't by intent, but my moment of heartache allowed her to show her strength. That's a trade-off I'm willing to make any day. It also reminded me that on my very worst day, I am still some child's best hope. We all are. Because too many of these kids have no hope at all.

On far too many occasions I have heard a young man or young woman proclaim, "Why should I care? No one else does."

The sheer, utter hopelessness of that singularly devastating statement hurts me more than any other. I have to let them know that it's not so. I have to let them know that I care. It's my responsibility as an educator, but it is also my responsibility as a human being. "I care," I tell them. "And if you can't think of any other reason to push yourself forward, realize that there is one person who does care. And that person is me."

They may not remember a single lesson that we teach them, but they will always remember how we made them feel. So why not make them feel hopeful, worthwhile, and necessary.

~ It's Not the Awards: It's the Rewards ~

AWARDS ARE NICE. Being voted "Teacher of the Year" symbolizes a teacher's commitment. A volunteer who receives an award for his or her efforts is surely flattered by the acclaim. But awards have a short-term life span. It is the rewards that drive us. Rewards are not plaques that you hang on the wall. A reward is Chris saying, "Ms. Goforth believes in me." It's Mary calling me from the hospital because she knows how much I care and trusts me enough to talk with her doctor on her behalf. It's a student running into my office shouting, "I got an *apple*, Ms. G."

Rewards translate into gratification, and gratification lasts a lifetime. Gratification is the thing upon which we measure our legacy. I want my legacy to read: She loved kids without question; she was always there for them.

If you look at our starfish, each attribute reflects a desire to make a difference in someone's life. That's why we're here.

~ Levi ~

IT IS NOT fair to say that any child is more precious or special than another, but if ever there was one, Levi would be it. "My Levi," I call him.

Levi was in the self-contained unit at Lee Junior High. His history is the kind that makes decent folks shudder. Calling Levi an abused child is an understatement of the most blatant kind. He spent much of his first seven years of life locked in a closet. He survived on a starvation diet. When he was finally discovered, he weighed 30 pounds and was teetering on death. His mental state was so deprived that the scars would never fully heal.

After his parents were arrested and charged, Levi found a home with a family that would spend years trying to repair the damage. Levi suffers from a condition not uncommon in children who have been systematically starved: he can never overcome the feeling of hunger. He will eat literally everything he can get his hands on. At school, it is essential that a teacher accompany him to lunch because he is driven to eat until he becomes sick, and then he still feels compelled to put something more in his mouth.

Levi was autistic, but he was also brilliant. One of his best tricks was reciting verbatim every word he had heard on television the previous night. His memory was absolute in that regard.

Coloring and coloring books were Levi's passions. And since I had just put a coloring program on one of the computers in my lab, I suggested to my principal and Levi's teacher that Levi spend one period a day in my classroom.

The class was instructive in other ways, as well. Everyone pitched in when it came to Levi. He learned to open files and access certain programs. One of his ongoing assignments was to type word for word the television commercials he had memorized during the week. Levi started to look forward to our class, so much so that one day he left his unit without permission and ran up and down the halls until he found the computer lab. He stormed into the room, scaring the kids half to death, and went straight to his chair, breathless and excited.

"Good afternoon, Levi," I said, trying to calm everyone.

"Hi, Ms. Goforth. I love you," he replied.

"I love you, too, Levi," I said. "Does your teacher know you're here?"

"No, ma'am," he admitted.

"Don't you think we should let her know?"

"No, ma'am. I like it here."

I sent one of my students to inform Levi's teacher that Levi was safe and sound and was in good hands. But then came the tricky part. I had to show Levi that there were always consequences to our actions, and that he couldn't just walk out of his class without facing up to the consequences. Levi had also discovered a new-found power in the words,

"I love you," but he also had to understand that using those words to avoid his responsibilities was unacceptable.

My students were not only fond of Levi, they were extremely protective of him. At some level they could empathize with all he had been through, since most of them had come up the hard way, as well. Levi provided them with a means of expressing this empathy and demonstrating compassion, not that they would have used those words. They were strong for him. They wanted him to do well. They were teaching him all the while he was teaching them about themselves. It was a remarkable dynamic.

~ Faith ~

I EXPERIENCED A similar dynamic some years back when I was providing foster care for kids. Faith was three years old when she came to me, a beautiful, battered, little girl who was so filled with attachment issues that she held on to me day and night.

I didn't feel right about leaving her at day care, so I arranged with my principal to bring her along to school. It was the gang kids who took to Faith most strongly. The connection was instantaneous. They helped me arrange a comfortable area next to my desk with her blanket and playthings. They crawled around with her, wrestled and played, and drew pictures. I didn't have to tell them that Faith had been physically abused. They could see the bumps and the bruises for themselves. I remember one of them asking her how it had happened, and I will never forget her reply or their reaction. When Faith replied, "Mommy did it. Mommy did it," I saw a wave of emotion roll over those kids with such power and such empathy that I was just glad Faith's "mommy" wasn't there; she may never have gotten out of that classroom alive.

These kids understood what had been taken from Faith; she was a three-year-old who might never trust again. She was starved for love; they knew the feeling and were determined to give it to her.

Faith and Levi were not isolated demonstrations of this empathetic dynamic. These were young men and women who had grown up with violence and poverty and had faced more dead ends in their short lives than most of us will ever know. And yet they never failed to show compassion for the mentally and physically challenged kids who came through our school. They would show a level of patience and understanding that never ceased to amaze me. They loved Levi. They didn't feel sorry for him. They loved Faith. They treated her with empathy, not sympathy, and she responded.

All I could do was step back and learn from them.

~ The Shape of Love ~

I TRULY BELIEVE that we come into this world with the capacity to love and with a desire to be loved. Our life experiences shape our view of love, sometimes for the better, but sometimes not.

The danger we all face – and certainly kids raised in dysfunctional families and in the throes of poverty are no exception – is that negative influences can adversely shape our perception of this most important and beautiful gift of love. They can distort our ability to love, and they can dampen our eagerness to be loved.

I have seen too many kids hardened by life, kids who build walls to protect themselves against any emotion, kids who neither believe nor trust, and kids who have found it easier to hate than to love.

After all, love is the greatest of all mysteries. Love makes us vulnerable, and yet love opens our hearts. Love is so often filled with conditions, and yet nothing makes the spirit soar the way love does. Love brings out our weaknesses, and yet it makes us strong beyond words. Some times love seems so hard, and yet it is really the easiest of all things to share.

If I have learned one thing, it is that love has to be unconditional. There can be no strings attached.

I volunteered some years back for a medical mission in Guatemala, and it proved to be one of the most inspiring times of my life. I worked at an orphanage for young girls. I didn't speak their language, and they surely did not speak mine. We were left with non-verbal communication. A smile, a gentle touch, a helping hand, a warm hug. I didn't have to say "I love you" to these girls. I felt it from the first moment we met. Some of them were more trusting than others, but it didn't take long for them to see that I had come to their country with the best intentions. My heart was open. I was willing to be vulnerable. They, on the other hand, only wanted some assurance that I was genuine. They were bursting with love. Their need for love was as obvious as their need to express it. I could see it in their eyes. In the end, what we shared without words left an indelible mark on my heart. Language was not an obstacle.

~ Jenny and Sue ~

DURING MY EARLY 20's, I actively participated in the foster care program sponsored by the state of Texas. In the course of those five astounding years, I had 28 different children residing for various lengths of time in my house. They ranged in age from 1 to 10. Since I lived close to the interstate highway, it wasn't unusual to receive a call at all hours of the day or night from the Highway Patrol.

This was typical of our conversations. "We've got a drunk driver on our hands, Debbie, and he has a two-year-old in the back seat. Can we bring her over?"

"Sure can." I always kept plenty of bologna and bubble bath close at hand because these itinerant souls were inevitably dirty and hungry. Little Tonya, the subject of that particular phone call, only stayed with me for two days. However, Jenny and Sue, two sisters, ages 4 and 7, were delivered to my door one harried summer evening at 1:00 a.m. and stayed for 18 months.

Sue was a pixie of a girl with a moon-shaped face and a lisp. Jenny's long, brown hair and tiny plastic barrettes were her signatures.

The girls' history was not pleasant. They were psychological basket cases. Their family, such as it was, was nothing short of a disaster. Their mother was a raging alcoholic. Their father had sexually abused them. The courts intervened for a time and refused to return the girls to this dysfunctional and dangerous situation.

Day by day, the girls and I grew closer. We were a fairy-tale family. We would eat pizza on Saturday and go to the playground on Sunday. My entire family adopted them. After 18 months, they were mine. And I was theirs. They were growing and changing and becoming healthy in mind and body. And then the roof caved in.

The parents returned to court. They both agreed to counseling, and their so-called marriage was dissolved. He agreed to move out of state and to never again have contact with the girls. Did this new living arrangement insure that their mother would forever be a reliable, loving parent? Did it guarantee that the abuse was over? No. But the court had no choice but to grant her custody of "my" girls.

I thought I was going to die. Never in my life did I face a more difficult moment than saying goodbye to Sue and Jenny. We had grown so close, and I loved them unconditionally. It wasn't that I felt like they were my girls; they were my girls. I had introduced them to so many things that they surely would never have experienced, including a regular church environment, playmates, and stability. I taught them to take pride in themselves. I taught them to think for themselves. I knew what kind of life they were returning to, and I could only hope that something of our time together would manifest over time and guide their steps.

This was, unfortunately, only partially true.

The girls contacted me twenty years later via Child Protection Services. Their lives had been troubled, to say the least. They had ended up once again living with their abusive father. Both girls had attempted suicide on more than one occasion. Both had married and divorced.

Jenny, however, did say the most profound thing, and I have always held on to the message behind her words. Her words have, in many ways, guided my teaching philosophy and my counseling methods. She said, "I'll never forget you. You loved us when no one else wanted us. I will always think of you as my mother because you gave me more in a year and a half than my birth mother ever did or ever will."

My years as a foster parent left me with an indelible image that fit those 28 kids, but also fits my at-risk kids today. It is a picture of young children in a mud puddle. In my mind, I pick each child up, wash them off, bring some stability to their lives, and then set them off again, to toddle into and out of more mud puddles. The image allowed me to let go of my foster children even though I had given them each my heart. My at-risk kids are no different and deserve no less. It's like learning to walk. At some point, they have to let go of your finger and try it on their own. The support that I gave them, that the best teachers and the most committed parents give them, has a lasting effect.

It makes picking yourself up easier. It makes dusting yourself off and heading toward that next mud puddle a less daunting task.

~ Unconditional ~

I CAN'T PICK and choose which kids I am going to care for or which kids are most deserving of my love. I can't give more to Mary than I do to Mona because I think one of them has a better chance of making good grades and being successful at the next level. I can't throw up my hands or turn my back on Chris even if I know he's bound for jail in a week. He deserves my best even if it's for one day or even if he walks away from me without a word.

I can't put conditions on my love for a child based upon behavior or potential or the scowl on his or her face. It's my job, yes, but it is also my responsibility as a human being. Who knows what effect a single moment of positive energy might have? Who knows what the ripple effect of a kind gesture might be? All I know is that a moment of positive energy is more effective than no energy at all, and a kind gesture goes a lot further than a cold shoulder.

A simple smile. A pat on the back. A positive word. A commitment to someone's self-worth. There is not one child alive who doesn't deserve these. Can I make an impact on every student I meet? Can I nudge every young man or woman who steps into my office a little closer to the light? Of course not.

I can't put conditions on my love or the depth of my compassion, but I also can't put expectations on the results. Some people might view that as a catch-22; I choose to see it as a fact of life. Relationships are like that.

Earlier we talked about Levi and the genuine affection that the most delinquent kids in school showed for him. Levi didn't see their tattoos. He didn't care that most of them had criminal records or had spent time in jail. Their rough language didn't put him off. All he cared about was the affection, the concern, and the regard they demonstrated for him. That was love in Levi's eyes, and the kids could feel the power of his love in return.

The at-risk kids who pass through my office every day have spent most of their lives hardening themselves against emotion. The further removed a child is from love, caring, and compassion, the more vulnerable they are. As I attempt to break down the impenetrable walls they have been hiding behind for so long, the first thing I become aware of is fear. Dropping your guard is scary. Opening yourself up is risky. The more you've been burned, the harder it is to recognize love, and the more difficult it is to accept it when it's offered. When you're starved for something genuine, the more distrustful you are of the feast that awaits you.

~ Love Them Anyway ~

THERE IS A lyric in a wonderful song by Martina McBride that goes like this, "You can spend your whole life building something from nothing. One storm can come and blow it all away. Build it anyway."

Then it goes on to say, "You can love someone with all your heart, for all the right reasons, and in a moment they can choose to walk away. Love them anyway."

For me, these are words to live by. They express so much about the relationship between teacher and student, mentor and apprentice, adult and child. Sometimes we give everything we have to give, and it's not enough. Sometimes we work our fingers to the bone and the effort goes unnoticed. Sometimes we go the extra mile, and the only reward we get is a small piece of self-satisfaction.

I have seen it so often in my roles as an educator and a "keeper of hope." Many times I have done everything in my power to help a student move a little closer to the light, to help him see his own potential, and to help him feel that ever-important measure of self-worth, and I lose him anyway. He returns to a life of drugs or chooses jail over school; he accepts failure over achievement, or he simply gives up on himself. But I can't allow that painful loss to cloud my vision for the next student. He or she may seem like a hopeless cause; I might know from the outset that the odds of making a difference are slim to none. I have to do it ANYWAY. I have to be that person – maybe the one and only person – who battles to the very end, who keeps the flame of hope burning, who believes without equivocation.

You and I can't stop believing in the children of this world no matter how beat down they might be or we might be.

Remember the Starfish poem at the beginning of this book? Remember the young man's determination to breathe life into as many starfish as possible by returning them to the sea?

Sometimes that starfish is going to wash ashore again. I still have to throw it back in the water. Like the song says, I do it anyway. I love them anyway. It's unconditional.

If we look again at the starfish that symbolizes the journey we have taken through these pages, we see that love lives at the center of the star. Love allows us to be approachable and to share compassion. Love makes us more potent communicators and more effective listeners. Love is what seeds our perseverance; it drives us to be more valuable role models. When we approach our work and our lives with a positive attitude, love enlivens us. When we offer our trustworthiness and pledge our dependability to the children of the world, love is both the foundation and the flower, the seed as well as the blossom.

Love is what drives us.

We are 'keepers of hope," and love is the fuel of our commitment. It is this love and the scars of love that define our success.

Scars are part of life's journey. Scars of love last forever.

To all "Keepers of Hope:" March on, march on! Never give up!

~ About Deborah Goforth ~

DEBBIE GOFORTH has been an educator and "keeper of hope" in the Texas school system since 1980, 27 years. She has taught at every level, but her primary focus has long been the tumultuous secondary school years. She has also coached girl's athletics, taught at the college level along with continuing education for adults, and been a teacher mentor. She has a Masters in Curriculum and Instruction. In 2003, she became an At-Risk Coordinator and turned to public speaking as a means of advocating for kids of all ages. Debbie has been promoting the phrase "No Child Will Be Left Behind" long before it came into vogue. She has been named Teacher of the Year numerous times, but it is not the awards but the rewards of seeing a child succeed that mean the most to her. *SCARS OF LOVE – Tears of Hope* is her first book.

Debbie is available for motivational speaking and for consulting services.

Contact:

Deborah Goforth

At-Risk Educational Services

P.O. Box 60286

San Angelo, TX 76906

(325) 227-5330

info@studentsatrisk.com

~ About Mark Graham ~

MARK GRAHAM is a critically acclaimed author who has been writing and editing professionally since 1988. He has collaborated with individuals from three continents on projects ranging from novels and biographies and to screenplays and business books on a variety of subjects. This is his first collaboration with Debbie Goforth.

He lives in Denver with his wife Nobuko and their three kids.

Please visit www.markgrahamcommunications.com for more.

To Order
Additional Copies of
Scars of Love – Tears of Hope

go to www.atlasbooks.com

~ About The Cover ~

The cover and interior pages of *Scars of Love – Tears of Hope* were designed and produced by Nick Zelinger of NZ Graphics. NZ Graphics also offers exceptional proofreading, copy editing services and superior design skills at affordable pricing.

For more information about book design and other services, visit www.nzgraphics.com